T0329281

The Rational Consumer:
Bad for Business and Politics
Democracy at the Crossroads of Nature and Culture

Francis B. Nyamnjoh

Langaa Research & Publishing CIG
Mankon, Bamenda

Publisher:
Langaa RPCIG
Langaa Research & Publishing Common Initiative Group
P.O. Box 902 Mankon
Bamenda
North West Region
Cameroon
Langaagrp@gmail.com
www.langaa-rpcig.net

Distributed in and outside N. America by African Books Collective
orders@africanbookscollective.com
www.africanbookcollective.com

ISBN-10: 9956-550-14-0

ISBN-13: 978-9956-550-14-2

Table of Contents

Foreword

Pierre Englebert

It is a credit to Francis Nyamnjoh's open-mindedness and tolerance (or is it his recklessness?) that he asked me to write a foreword to *The Rational Consumer: Bad for Business and Politics – Democracy at the Crossroads of Nature and Culture*, his latest volume in an already long and rich publication list. The request left me much flattered but also puzzled and – paradoxically for a book largely on reason – questioning his own rationality. Truth be told, I am an ignoramus next to him and largely incompetent in the matters the book addresses. I cannot comment on the Freudian and post-Freudian psychology that sits at the core of the argument with even an ounce of proficiency, nor do I know much about public relations theory. And while I live in the middle of the American mayhem he discusses, I do not study it and have little insightful to say about it, save for sharing the grief I experience like many of us.

And yet, I feel I can maybe contribute something the reader might find useful, for Francis's book left me inspired, provoked in the best sense of the word and full of reactions, like an eager student in a first-year seminar. Yes, whatever context or discipline one comes from, there is much to learn from this book, which is erudite but in no way inaccessible. Its beautiful prose – as always with Francis – is hospitable to the reader. Even if post-Freudian psychology is not your cup of tea, you will not regret going along for the ride because democracy, liberalism and what makes our humanity (individually and socially) are the real topics of this book, and they certainly are everyone's concerns.

Subjectively, a few points among many struck me and might whet others' appetites for reading. The first is the question that buttresses the book: What is the individual freedom to vote if it is based on emotional manipulation? How free are we? One cannot but be left very uncomfortable and forced to introspection at Francis's words: "democracy becomes exaggeratedly little more than suspending rationality and relentlessly pandering to the hidden, complex, layered and ever-multiplying desires of the elusive individual who seeks freedoms without many responsibilities in return" (p.78).

Second is Francis's pointed questioning of the origin of the belief that democracy is only compatible with capitalism. For sure, there are strong philosophical foundations to this claim that predate Freud and the empirical evidence – notwithstanding measurement problems that might be self-fulfilling – of the relationship between the two, over time and space, appear robust. Yet, Francis suggests that it is also the result of purposeful and methodical manipulation based on the insights of Freudian analysis, a sort of Gramscian hegemonic thinking that leaves us largely unable to look more critically into it. As someone who studied Economics in American academia, I can confirm that a discipline that vaunts its own rationality and empiricism largely takes its own assumptions as articles of faith.

The reader who, like me, tends to think of herself as somewhat rational cannot help but feel provoked. Going even further, Francis asks to what extent rational liberal individualism, a system so many of us still cherish, might actually be the genetic ancestor of the untruth system that has dominated American politics these last few years.

Francis Nyamnjoh has a gift for the salutary intellectual provocation. His recent text on *Rhodes Must Fall*, in which he challenged South African xenophobia for its Rhodesian reproduction, was a powerful case in point. His notion that Rhodes did not fall but was merely taking a stroll around the neighbourhood brought up Francis's formidable sense of humour, his analytical perceptiveness and a call for humility in the face of our certainties. In a different context, *The Rational Consumer* furthers this intellectual agenda.

In the United States of America, we are fond of using social sciences, our material development and our rationality, as foundations to study other societies. We often find their democracies and their modernisation wanting, short of some standard inspired by an idealised version of ourselves and of where we stand. In this compelling book, Francis Nyamnjoh turns the mirror back on us. It is an unsettling experience, but one that has the potential to enlighten.

Claremont, California
2 July 2018

Introduction

A certain age-old, stubborn question about human nature is in no hurry to leave us. Put quite simply, the question is to what extent the human being, at the state of nature, should be credited with a sense of morality. A second question is, how much can that human nature be transformed (corrected or corrupted) by belonging to a society (ideal or real) with a clear set of values, a practised sense of direction, a well-oiled morality and an ethics of mutuality? Is the state of nature to be cultivated and domesticated in the interest of a status quo (contrived or consensual, negotiated or assumed) or kept away from the purportedly corrupting influences of established society and taken-for-granted albeit problematic orders of things?

Put differently, the tension between a human being acting in pursuit of personal interests in full autonomy (motivated or not by reason, emotion or both), and a human being acting in solidarity with other human beings in pursuit of common goals and shared interests undergirded by shared principles and values remains largely unresolved, even as it has fired up many a social engineer with sleepless nights throughout the history of humankind as active agents.

When the need to cultivate nature is emphasised in the interest of one collectivist, societal or civilisational objective or another, it has not always been easy to establish just how much cultivation of nature is necessary, desirable or even possible. Often, the tendency has been to make or stake a claim and act in tune with it until a contradiction surfaces, forcing one to concede that human nature is complex, and that to cultivate or to socialise is to make choices about group membership, belongingness and value systems in conversation with nature, human and environmental. Thus, sending one back to the drawing board to explore alternative relationships and configurations between nature and culture, freedom and subjection, autonomy and collective consciousness and action, independence and dependence, individual and society, particularism and universalism, us and them, self and other, me and you.

This notwithstanding, much of the thinking on human nature and relationships is perplexingly dichotomous. It leaves little room for an accommodating and nuanced perspective informed by an appreciation of the complexity of being human in a nonzero-sum manner and in contexts of *Ubuntu-ism*, where being called upon to choose amounts to a challenge to seek to include as much and as many as one possibly can (Nyamnjoh 2015; 2017[2015]b).

Equally dichotomous and pitched in terms of binary oppositions has been the debate about the place and power of rationality and irrationality, reason and emotion, mind and body, brain and heart, in human action and interaction. People are presented as either rational or irrational, thoughtful or passionate, active or passive in disposition. The dominant scholarly attitude and approach is perplexingly one of giving up even before making an effort at putting together what at face value nature or its (omniscient, omnipotent and omnipresent) creator might have put asunder. Not factored in at all or factored in only sparingly is the possibility that in real life circumstances, in the pursuit of individual or collective self-interest, people are both rational and irrational, thoughtful and passionate, active and passive, depending on the context, the relationship in question and the issues at stake. If rational behaviour is that which serves to maximise the self-interest of an individual, a group or a society, why should one exclude a priori behaviour and action driven by emotions that yield maximum outcome for the self-interest of the individual, group or society concerned? A blind and stubborn insistence on the purity and sanctity of apparent divisions or chasms between reason and emotion (and all that are associated with either) ought really to be seen as an excuse to control through claims and denials of social visibility as a technology of power, status and privilege. Thus, for example, just by accusing an individual of being overly emotional and of being governed more by the heart than by the mind is reason enough to deny that individual the social visibility and status that makes possible claims to power and privilege, or to have a say in public affairs. This logic could be and has easily been extended as a blanket of inclusion and exclusion based on hierarchies of humanity and rationality informed by such considerations as race, geography, culture, class, gender, age and sex. The assumption being that the higher up the hierarchies, the more rational and therefore the more entitled is an individual or group to power, privilege, ownership and control over fellow humans and over the natural and supernatural resources of the world.

In view of all these dichotomous and zero-sum assumptions, if only reason or rationality were less of a front and more of a genuine aspiration, one could ask if it wouldn't be more realistic – closer to the state of things as they actually are, as opposed to how we imagine they ought to be – to seek to ensure balance or, at the very least, fair representation for nature and culture, acting on and being acted upon by others, emotion and reason or logic, mind and body, brain and heart, rationality and irrationality? If being both natured and cultured, active and passive, rational and irrational in thought and action are part and parcel of being human through relationships with fellow humans and with the worlds of nature and supernature, how could we overly emphasise and advantage the one without equally overly de-emphasising and jeopardising the other and the needed balance of being human?

If it is normal and attractive to invest in raw unadulterated emotion (feelings, desires, affect, passions, the heart) as both the corporate world and the world of politics would suggest, and as their consultants in the media and among psychologists and public relations practitioners would agree, why have some civilisations – those usually labelled as "Western" – tended to be packaged, presented and sold to the rest of the world as *Civilisations of Exceptions* in which reason and the rational trumps emotion and the irrational? In what way could such a civilisation convincingly extricate itself from the charge of keeping up appearances about the triumph of reason, logic and science, while actually relying on superstition, irrationality and emotion as its technologies of daily articulation, sustenance and reproduction? And what are we to make of the fact that the West and the Western have always used as excuse for their penetration and conquest of other peoples, societies, geographies and regions of the world, accusations of the latter of living under the shadowy canopy of irrationality, savagery and the reign of terror by dangerous passions and volcanic emotions? To what intellectual ancestry could we attribute this particular dualism and perception of nature and culture as layered and hierarchical in its virtues and dangers?

There was Sigmund Freud. He was born in 1856 in Příbor, Czech Republic, and died in 1939 in Hampstead, United Kingdom. At the centre of this conversation are his fears and concerns about human nature, and the impossibility of civilisation as a zero-sum game of absolutes – an enterprise of absolute winners and absolute losers. How could any society claim to be truly civilised when it is impossible to fully harness the caprice of human nature? How could any measure of rationality be confidently claimed, when it could always be surprised at every turn of its progression by rebellious snipers from the confederate army of the dark forces of nature it supposedly defeated to claim a premature "victory" of light over darkness? Freud, through his analysis of dreams and free associations and of individual and group psychology (Freud 2010[1931], 1949), first advanced the argument that hidden deep inside the dark tropical jungles of our minds, and

4

rumbling like lava in a volcano, are repressed, dangerous instinctual drives and primitive sexual and aggressive animalistic forces, the unleashing of which could result in the cannibalisation of social order by the devastating barbarism of such forces. Freud's ideas gave licence to see ordinary people as driven not by their minds but by their basic instincts. Whether acting as individuals or as part of a crowd, the result was the same. Basically, the action was characterised by unreason, irrationality and instinctive animality. It was action that exuded all that is uncultivated, untamed and undomesticated about the human being. In other words, it was the dangerous anti-social action of the human still subjected to the tempestuousness and monstrous instincts of the state of nature. The only way the potential for chaos and destruction in individuals and societies could be tamed or neutralised was to explore ways of keeping in check (monitoring and controlling) such dangerous forces. His major concern was how to liberate people and civilisation from such dangerous subterranean drives.

This essay takes a closer look at how psychologists, as archaeologists of the mind and basic human instincts, have applied Freud's theory of the unconscious in seeking answers to the conundrum highlighted above. It discusses, as well, how Freud's ideas have been distilled and applied by public relations agents in the interest of big business (corporations) to promote consumerism, and by politicians to seek and maintain power through targeted political campaigns, elections and a semblance of democracy (Herman and Chomsky 1988; Chomsky 1989, 2002; Tye 1998). This entire analysis is inspired by, draws from and feeds into insights articulated in a four part 2002 BBC television documentary by Adam Curtis, *The Century of the Self*, to which I am deeply indebted. Hardly could Freud have anticipated the uses to which his theory, ideas and insights would be put by corporations and politicians in the 20th and 21st centuries. The popularity of his theory of the unconscious would only further accelerate with added complexity following the explosion in creative innovation made possible by advances in technologies of mass communication and social networking, and especially because of the insidious godlike capacities in these technologies for presence in simultaneous multiplicities. The essay is thus structured around the contested application of Freud's theory in the emotional manipulation of people by the hidden or not so hidden persuaders (Packard 1981[1957]) actively promoting the idea and ideals of a consumer society underpinned by consumer capitalism and consumer democracy (Jones 1965; Goodwin et al. 1997). In addition to these introductory remarks, the essay consists of five other parts, namely: (2) captured by subterranean forces; (3) Freud adopted and adapted for consumerism by Edward Bernays; (4) the rational consumer: bad for business and politics; (5) freedom at last or wolves of repression in sheepskin?; and (6) conclusion: beyond impoverishing dichotomies.

2

Captured by Subterranean Forces

Seen through the prism of Freud's unconscious mind, built into modernity, civilisation and democracy are their nemesis – each contains within itself the hidden and not so hidden forces for its very own self-destruction. No society, whatever its level of sophistication and development can fully escape the submerged dangerous forces lurking beneath the surface – forces that could erupt easily to produce a frenzied mob with the power to undo governments and humble any pretentions to the very values it claims and celebrates (e.g. democracy and civilisation). The idea of hidden dangers depicted by Freud is at variance with a basic assumption in democracy that human beings could be trusted to make rational decisions in predictable ways, and to make coexistence possible through robust public debate of ideas and options informed by competing and complementary societal and political visions (Habermas 1989; Goode 2005; Johnson 2006; McChesney and Nichols 2016). If irrationality seems the order of the day even as the rhetoric may be that of rational choices, logical and predictable behaviour, what is there to stop smart salesmen and saleswomen seeking to engineer consent through developing and championing psychological techniques for managing and controlling the unconscious feelings of the unsuspecting masses (Herman and Chomsky 1988; Chomsky 1989, 2002; Tye 1998)? And if humans were basically controlled by animal or unconscious instinctual drives lurking beneath the surface of civilisation, then psychology as the archaeology of the mind would be the science par excellence for understanding the mechanisms by which the individual and popular mind works, specifically with the goal of figuring out how to apply those mechanisms into strategies for social control.

In Adam Curtis's *The Century of the Self*, we are given a complex and sophisticated account of just how Freud's ideas of individual and group psychology and of dangerous unconscious forces have been appropriated by powerful corporations and politicians – especially and quite paradoxically in purported democratic societies such as the United States of America (USA) and the United Kingdom (UK) – to seek to control individuals, groups and crowds, and to strengthen the grip on power of the political, economic and cultural elite (Harrison and Madge 1987; Harrison 2011[1976]; Hubble 2006). Produced in 2002, *The Century of the Self* depicts practices that predated and offer an instructive background for understanding the 2016 *liaison dangereuse* between Facebook[2] and Cambridge Analytica (a client of Facebook), involving the misappropriation of the personal data of over 87 million American voters seen to have tipped the election in favour of Donald J. Trump. Cambridge Analytica, – a firm linked to former Trump adviser Steve Bannon (Green 2017; Koffler 2017)[3] – compiled user data to target American voters,[4] and in the process proved its willingness to go to extreme lengths, however unethical, to serve the propaganda and ideological interests of its clients and sponsors by providing campaign themes informed by meticulous analyses of various psychological value and lifestyle profiles across a myriad of social networks (Watts 2018).[5] Cambridge Analytica was also revealed to have been involved with the 2017 Kenyan elections, as a consultant for the presidential candidate who won the controversial elections, Uhuru Kenyatta. According to a report by Jina Moore in the *New York Times*, Mark Turnbull, a Cambridge Analytica executive, boasted how: "the company twice rebranded Mr. Kenyatta's political party, wrote his campaign speeches and his political platform, and twice conducted surveys of 50,000 people to ascertain Kenyan voters' hope and fears"[6]. Note the emphasis on the emotions of hope and fear as drivers of elections, and how little or nothing is said or hinted at on rational choices through the force of thoughtful and logical debates with an interest in distilling the truth of Kenyan politics and society, and promoting values and political action that favour national integration and unity in diversity. Like mercenaries, Cambridge Analytica seemed more interested in assisting the capture of power by their clients than in assuming and ensuring, as well, the ethical responsibilities of what actually is done with that power. Equally noteworthy is the role played by psychologists and psychometry in the development of online data-mining techniques (Laterza 2018; Watts 2018).[7] Although Cambridge Analytica shut down in May 2018 and filed for bankruptcy, blaming a "siege of media coverage" that had "driven away virtually all of the company's customers and suppliers," few would be surprised if the company re-emerges "in some other incarnation or guise".[8] For few, especially among the ruling elite, are inclined to give up easily on the idea of hidden persuaders using psychological techniques of subtle persuasion to craft winning formulae and deliver easy victories by playing on and mining people's hidden desires and fears (Packard 1981[1957]: 232–239). It is simply irresistible for powermongers to ignore or give up on cyberspace as a battleground of choice for propaganda, cannibalisation of the masses and fanning the runaway flames of soaring greed and autocracy (Sanger 2018; Watts 2018).[9] Given how much we can learn about "what people really think, what they really want, and what they really do", and in view of the fact that there is "almost no limit to what can be learned about human nature" from Big Data, if we ask the right questions (Stephens-Davidowitz 2017: 158), it is difficult to envisage the political and economic elite turning a blind eye on such a potent and tempting reservoir of wealth and power. Data mining is here to stay, we may well conclude (Watts 2018), even as we recognise the threat to democracy that comes with the systematic, harmful and misleading manipulation of data and "relentless targeting of hyper-partisan views, which play to the fears and prejudices of people, in order to influence their voting plans".[10]

As Edward Bernays discusses at length in the preface to the new edition of his book, *Crystalizing Public Opinion* (Bernays 1961[1923]: iii–lvi), public opinion has not always found favour with leaders through history, even when presenting itself as "capable of being wooed and won by leaders" (Bernays 1961[1923]: xii). Some leaders seek and maintain power through the purported blue blood of royalty and/or by the brute force of dictatorship and autocracy. They do not hesitate to use the barrel of the gun and blinkering personality cults to evoke fear, energise the desire to hate and extract unconditional respect and loyalty from the cowed populace. They hate to pander to the masses and distrust everything remotely suggestive of meaningful freedoms from the perspective of those masses. They identify with what Barack Obama has termed "strongman politics", in which a semblance of democracy is maintained, while "those in power seek to undermine every institution or norm that gives democracy meaning", by absolutely insisting on dictating reality.[11] Like the fascist dictators of Europe between 1919 and 1945 such as Hitler, Stalin and Mussolini (Wiskemann 1966; Snyder 2017, 2018; Albright 2018) and the absolute monarchs before them (Beloff 1954), these leaders would find in Nicolo Machiavelli's *The Prince* (1992) a trusted and worthy companion in their daily journeys of navigation and negotiation of the enchanting intricacies of autocratic power. Cambridge Analytica type market research and public opinion polls conducted by such leaders tend to be strictly factual in the questions asked, as the overriding concern is far less one of taking heed of how the populace feel and what they desire than know what they think in order best to police those thoughts. The leaders are keen on spotting the way the wind of public opinion blows much more in order to contain and forestall than to enable and encourage. With such leadership it is seldom a question of giving the people what they want. It is taken for granted that, as leaders, they know what is best for their people, and should enjoy uncontested authority and unfettered powers. It is a leadership much more interested in conquest and the art of winning without being right by nipping at the bud any sign of discontent by silenced masses and subjects (Browder 2015; Snyder 2017, 2018; Albright 2018; Frum 2018; Mcfaul 2018). Other leaders, on their part, seek to win and keep the affection of the people by appealing to the positive feelings and desires in them. Fear and terror as a technology of power and government are minimised. Seen through the prism of Freudian ideas and ideals, the logic of this approach is that if leaders are able to use the rule of law, public institutions and loyalty to common ideals to harness the libidinal forces or primordial bonds of love and desire for themselves and their projects, while unleashing on purported outsiders and on their enemies the aggressive instincts of those over whose destinies they preside, they are more likely to be able to control and harness the otherwise unpredictable forces lurking within their fellow citizens or subjects (McCain 2018; Comey 2018; Dionne Jr. et al. 2017).[12]

Although emotions are as common an attribute of being human as is the capacity to think and to reason, there is a tendency to consider thought as rational and to be encouraged, and emotion as irrational and dangerous. The mind and its activities are appreciated while the body, its needs and desires are to be ignored, frowned upon or reduced to a bare minimum of attention. The result is often a systematic attempt in power relations to manage emotions by subduing or rendering them invisible, in order to keep up the appearance of being powerful and in control of oneself, of others and of situations. To those in worldly power, with sharpened ambitions of supremacy and dominance, and seeking to be firmly in charge, the control that comes with analysing one's inner feelings is something to be done to lesser and weaker dependent others, not something to contemplate for oneself. In their eyes, power should be beyond the reach of emotion, and thus to be nourished entirely by reason and perceived as always reasonable and right. To even entertain the idea of looking inwards and seeking to tame the monsters within the anatomy of those in power is not only treated by them and those who prop them up as embarrassing. It is also regarded as a threat to the absolute control one in power should have over one's body and the appetites it inspires, and also to those over whom one is supposed to exercise power.

If those in power show themselves to be weak, however indirectly, they see themselves as running the risk of losing that power. So, even when they do indulge in the temptations of the flesh and succumb to the weaknesses of the body – i.e. when they admit that "we are all human" in the manner of someone who has fallen from grace, they must do all in their power and privilege to keep this a secret, to hush things up, including buying and killing (known as "catch and kill") potentially compromising stories, if necessary.[13] Boys don't cry, we hear every now and again, and boys who yield easily to the lure and allure of their emotions, are urged to control themselves, or to hush up those who have tempted them with the pleasuring weakness of being. Girls in power, on the other hand, can only be taken seriously if they are able to assert their boyishness of being, through tomboy-like self-affirmation to earn accolades such as Margaret Thatcher's "Iron Lady" nickname. A girl with ambitions of power who expresses her feelings, making known for example that she is unhappy in her relationships with men – be these her father, brother, husband or simply an acquaintance – is thought of as displaying a weakness incommensurate with being in a position of power and showing leadership. Shedding tears, for whatever reason, with or without a shoulder to cry on, is seen as tantamount to weakness and a loss of respect. Iron-fists, iron-ladies and stiff upper lips are called for in a world configured narrowly around and championed by a conquering supremacist masculinity and its diktats.

At the heart of Freud's theory of the unconscious is an emphasis on self-control, and on keeping one's feelings or emotions in check, both for the good of the individual concerned and the stability of the society of which he or she is a part. Within the Freudian frame of things, if one is physically and emotionally abused with reckless abandon, it is considered beneath one and unsettling to the established order of things to erupt in anger or display unhappiness in public. One only needs to take a look at the bad press in mainstream media that has usually accompanied mass movements such as "Black Lives Matter" in the USA, UK and South Africa, for evidence of how much the emotion of anger tends to be castigated and treated as a far worse sin than the enslavement, colonialism, exploitation and dispossession at the root of such anger and protest movements (Nyamnjoh 2016). To be well brought up in Freud's days and terms, and still very much in many a 21st century community – despite notable significant shifts to accommodate the private and public display of emotion – is to be bottled up as well. To keep an unbreakable seal or lid over one's internal volcanoes continues to be perceived as a sign of strength of character. Wanted are contained and predictably nonporous people very properly doing the right things and living the proper life. While the lower classes cannot always afford the luxury of containing or enveloping themselves because of the sheer magnitude of the abuses they suffer from power and privilege gone wild, the powerful, on their part, invest in doing everything to hide away from the public their monstrosities, even if they do not always succeed. Often, they are driven to indulge themselves in a double life – one public (full of stiff upper lip and puritanical pretences) and the other more private and secretive (when they can let themselves go with the knowledge that they are not being preyed upon by the judgemental flames of the public gaze). It is to live a split personality not dissimilar to the story of the disciplined, tamed, peace-loving and personable Dr Jekyll and his violent, criminal-minded opposite, Mr Hyde. Both are characters in Robert Louis Stevenson's 1886 novella, *Strange Case of Dr Jekyll and Mr Hyde*. However, even if this understanding of rationality is difficult to attain, it is arguably still a desirable standard to set. Democracy does require self-control, especially in the sense that when there is conflict, we resolve it through political means as opposed to going on a murderous rampage in the manner of a Mr Hyde. In the absence of rationality as a check on our desires, society as a fair system of cooperation might not even be possible.

Could the occasional scandals (usually around sexuality and sexual affairs – libidinal in Freudian terms) that hit the high and mighty (royalty, top politicians, CEOs of corporations, celebrities, etc.) be indicative of the fact that however much has changed, the tendency to carry along with us the dregs and debris of our self-cultivation and civilisational endeavours is a constant reminder that it is extremely difficult, if not impossible, to permanently separate Dr Jekyll from his or her evil twin, Mr or Ms Hyde? Is it expecting too much to urge and expect people to control their basic instincts and impulses? Could it be that we overreact by being so over-the-top with our embarrassment at the fact that our impulsive animal nature is not in a hurry to part company with our assumed rational persona? Socialisation and the cultivation of the self, however thorough, cannot always corrode, erase or undo the instinctual and less than rational dimensions of being human. If neuroscience is to be believed, the Silicon Valley of our nature is a veritable birthmark and lifelong hidden persuader. Paradoxical as it might seem, the very success of any socialisation or cultivation of the self depends on just how effective the infrastructure and mechanisms of legitimation are able to carry along these other supposedly shady dimensions of the aspiring humans. The darkness of being human is never far away from its enlightenment; the one seems always to shadow or bodyguard the other in their entanglement or Siamese-ness of being. Could the promotion of violence through war and sports, for example, be a form of catharsis by the ruling and privileged classes to rediscover, even if only through the lesser creatures they preside over, the raw forms of emotiveness they have been forced to tame or pretend to distance themselves from?

Wittingly or not, Freud, by encouraging his patients to examine their innermost selves the way his theory of the unconscious suggested, also contributed to making his patients question many taken-for-granted things and ideas about society and social practices. With such questioning, his patients and others exposed to his thinking would begin to rethink and contest ideas of civilisation, progress, empire and grandeur that they had internalised and tended to reproduce and normalise with little or no critical interrogation. In his book, *Civilisation and its Discontents* (1957), Freud attacks the idea that civilisation is an expression of human progress. He argues, on the contrary, that if anything, civilisation has actually been constructed to control the instinctual and irrational propensities of the human being. Civilisation and its civilities, in other words, are meant to create a false sense of rationality, happiness and docility among its casualties and malcontents by creating and propagating the impression that it is achievable for human beings to completely divorce themselves from instinctual drives that have come to be associated with the raw or natural dimensions of their being. That said, in purely philosophical terms, however, if one were to follow thinkers who have sought to distinguish between positive and negative freedom, the Freudian attempt to control our instinctual, irrational self could be seen as a sign of human freedom and progress. According to this logic, whereas animals are not free because they act purely in accordance with instinct – at least so humans wish and tend to think – human beings are free because they act in accordance with their representation of laws of nature. It is consistent with the notion of freedom as self-determination, according to which an irrational life is a determinate existence in which nature, not one, is really the cause of one's action (Berlin 2002). Seen in these terms, civilisation does signify some sort of progress, if the starting point is that humans were once animals who have now acquired the ability to change or unshackle themselves from nature and the animalistic dimensions of their being. But just how realistic is it to argue that people can truly divorce themselves from nature to be able to consistently and systematically respond in authentic ways to the facticity of their everyday existence regardless of context and the nature of the relationship in question? A second problem with this train of thought is that humans and only humans are doing the assessments of progress, with no animals in sight to say whether or not they agree and why.[14]

It could be argued that the often celebrated individual freedom at the heart of democracy, for example, is patently impossible, a pure illusion, as human beings could never be truly afforded the freedom to express themselves because any unshackled freedoms are considered too dangerous by the instances of legitimation of given civilisations, societies and social orders. To discipline to the point of punishment is the order of the day, even in so-called democracies. This might account for why individuals would always be discontent, whatever illusions of happiness are daily paraded in front of them or dished out to them as palliatives.[15] Captured on the one hand by dangerous subterranean forces of the unconscious mind and constantly placated by the overbearing control of the truly powerful, the ordinary and not so ordinary folks of any given society that lays claim to democratic credentials, make as little sense of democracy in real terms as do patients subjected to daily doses of feel-good medication to relieve themselves of an immediate pain or an immediate yearning, while doing little to alleviate the root cause of the pain. Far from seeking truly equitable power relations, any pretensions to democracy seek little more than to maintain deeply hierarchical and repressive structures of power, even if this necessitates feeding the public with placebos of freedom in order to keep them happy, docile and amenable to manipulation. If a way could be found to keep the irrational and unconscious minds of the public stimulated, then the truly powerful of any given society could basically continue with the business of lording over or playing God in the lives of others. This is the case even or perhaps especially in the USA, where, despite its credentials as the global gendarme of freedom and democracy,[16] the prosperous elite few have developed and seemingly perfected techniques and mechanisms of keeping the restless many in their place[17] and a truly participatory democracy a distant dream (Mills 1956; Marcuse 2002[1964]; Herman and Chomsky 1988; Chomsky 1989, 1999, 2002, 2004; Barsamian 1994a, 1994b; Tye 1998; McChesney 2013, 2015; McChesney and Nichols 2016). A situation which begs the question: How could the citizens of a world power be made to feel so powerless about harnessing their country and its power in the interest of the majority, without, a priori, having the majority harnessed by instinctual forces?

3

Freud Adopted and Adapted for Consumerism by Edward Bernays

As *The Century of the Self* reveals, it was not Freud who personally marketed his ideas amongst the economically and politically powerful forces of society. Freud developed his theory mainly in Vienna, Austria, where he lived, but it was in the USA that his ideas would be first adopted, adapted and popularised. The link was Freud's American nephew, Edward Bernays, who was born in 1891 in Vienna, Austria, and who died in 1995 in Cambridge, Massachusetts, USA (Tye 1998).[18] Bernays's "mother was Freud's sister, and his father's sister was Freud's wife," which gave him "an intimate connection to the Father of Psychoanalysis, a connection he capitalized on every chance he got." He was fascinated, from conversations with his uncle, about Freud's novel ideas on "how unconscious drives dating to childhood make people act the way they do", and "was convinced that understanding the instincts and symbols that motivate an individual could help him shape the behavior of the masses" (Tye 1998: 8–9). Bernays was not a psychoanalyst, but he kept the company of many, including that of Anna Freud, his uncle's youngest daughter. Tye notes that Bernays was "one of Freud's most faithful students and most frequent imitators", even if he did not always acknowledge it, and although "he was more preoccupied with the public arena while Freud was captivated by matters private and inward-looking" (Tye 1998: 197). Bernays capitalised on his uncle's theory, by becoming the first person to use, however misguidedly and opportunistically, Freud's ideas in mass manipulation and persuasion. Recognising the monetary and historical value of Freud's writings to both Freud and himself, Bernays personally promoted the publication, reading and popularisation of Freud's books in the USA in the 1920s, for which he harvested significant royalties on his uncle's behalf (Tye 1998: 185–197). To Tye, the relationship between the two "was more complex and mutually enriching than was apparent to outsiders" (Tye 1998: 189). In his creative and opportunistic appropriation of Freud's ideas, Bernays was later to be considered to have influenced the 20th century nearly as much as did his uncle, each for his distinctive contribution to a field, its methods and practice. "[W]hile Freud sought to liberate people from their subconscious drives and desires", Bernays "sought to exploit those passions" (Tye 1998: 197). Freud is remembered as "the father of psychoanalysis" and Bernays as "the father of public relations" or "the father of spin" (Tye 1998: 227–228).[19] According to Tye, by his death in 1995 at the age of 103, Bernays had made a compelling case to be called "the prince of publicity", ensuring that this would be lost to no one who cared to research and read up on public relations by "leaving to the Library of Congress more than eight hundred boxes of personal and professional papers that detailed cases he'd worked on and tactics and strategies he'd employed over a career that spanned eight decades" (Tye 1998: viii–x). He would thus have been proud with his obituary, the first paragraph of which proclaimed him "an early leader in the public relations field who devised or developed many techniques for influencing public opinion", and acknowledged "his niche in cultural history" (Tye 1998: 227).

Freud discovered the unfathomable hidden powers of the unconscious in the workings of the human mind, while Bernays cashed in on the discovery. Freud's ideas had inspired Bernays to develop and perfect the art of utilising "publicity … to bring about social control by government of industrial activities, as well as for stimulating the interest of the public in an individual or organization, and building goodwill" (1961[1923]: xxvii). Bernays harnessed the powers of Freud's theory of the unconscious mind in the interest of the dominant economic and political elite of the USA. To uncover the secret self of the American consumer (and subsequently the American voter), Bernays was interested to find out why people behaved the way they did, bought what they bought, responded to advertising the way they did and voted the way they did in elections. People were not always the most adept at self-knowledge. There were unconscious sexual, psychological, sociological and/or cultural motivations that they were not always aware of that shaped the choices people made about what they bought and consumed, and how they voted. He was so successful in doing this that he is largely credited with inventing the science and practice of public relations (Bernays 1952; The F. W. Faxon Company 1951) or "spin doctoring" (Tye 1998),[20] along with Ivy Lee (Bernays 1961[1923]: xxxviii; Tye 1998: 227–249).[21] By public relations, Bernays understood:

(1) information given to the public, (2) persuasion directed at the public to modify attitudes and actions, and (3) efforts to integrate attitudes and actions of an institution with its publics and of publics with those of that institution (1961[1923]: lv).

Bernays's creative innovation brought Freud's theory of the unconscious into the heart of advertising and marketing – the age-old industry of sell and spin by tapping into desire and creating need with fantasies of narcissism, freedom, virility and much beyond, an industry which, with his input, would transform consumption and consumerism into a religion that defies the confines of race, place, class, age, sex, culture, language and competing religions (Miller 1995, 2012).[22] He emphasised the importance of applied psychological theory as an essential part of how corporations, and subsequently politicians, were going to appeal to their publics effectively. By encouraging corporations and politicians to invest in understanding the motivations of the human mind, Bernays was able, in regular consultation with practising psychologists, to help them package, sell and spin their consumer products and political platforms to their target consumers and electorates respectively (Bernays 1961[1923], 2004[1928], 1947, 1952; Tye 1998). To achieve this end, Bernays was ready to join American corporations in waging war against competing and conflicting ideologies, not only within the USA, but beyond its borders as well. This, for example, explains the carefully engineered propaganda "war of words and symbols" Bernays waged against the socialist government of Guatemala in 1954, on behalf of one of America's richest companies, the United Fruit Company (Tye 1998: 1955–1983). Both the US government of the day, eager to keep communism at bay, and the US media which Bernays expertly manipulated, were complicit in the war. "Bernays helped mastermind that war for his fruit company client, drawing on all of the public relations tactics and strategies he'd refined over forty years" to shape public opinion in America, Guatemala and globally by being deliberately deceptive, economical with the facts and generally manipulative of the situation on the ground in Guatemala (Tye 1998: 155–156).

Initially, Bernays achieved his end by demonstrating to corporations in America for the first time how they could make the public want things that they did not really need by linking mass-produced goods to the unconscious desires of the individuals targeted by the products. Bernays had discovered how his uncle's ideas of the unconscious mind could be used to drum up business and rattle people with insatiable appetites and burning desires, that could set them hunting and thirsting after the imagined solutions dangled before them by advertisers and public relations agents working for corporations as well as for politicians and political parties. The consuming public in turn was made to appreciate the therapeutic and confidence-boosting dimensions of identifying with a given product, and that it was the right thing to do not only for their personal health, but also for the wellbeing of their society. Consumer loyalty was as much an act of personal self-fulfilment as it was a duty to one's society as a citizen. It showed that individuals were patriotic and in tune with the values, expectations and ambitions of their society (Bernays 1961[1923], 2004[1928], 1947, 1952; Packard 1981[1957]; Tye 1998).

A new political idea of how to control the electorate and the public was born, and with it the consuming self. Just by being able to satisfy people's inner desires or at least making believe that one could, an individual, a politician, a political party or a corporation was well placed to make sleeping dogs lie happily in tranquillity and perfect docility. Consumed by a numbing happiness and agreeable submissiveness, the consuming self was hardly in a position to question the rise and enshrinement of the illusion of consumer sovereignty driven by and excelling in rational choices. Not only would the consuming self in turn consumed by stupor become the heart of the economy, it would also be disciplined by expectations of happiness and Pavlovian submissiveness in order to bring about and maintain the manageable and stable society which the United States of America aspired to be. The illusion of powerless or benevolent corporations working nonstop to satisfy every whim and caprice of their powerful queen-mother consumer – the happy, docile and spoilt consumer – went hand in hand with an equally potent illusion powered by an exaggerated and mostly unsubstantiated sense of rational choice and individual autonomy. However, despite the apparent happiness and docile placidity, just beneath the surface one could unearth much greater unhappiness and much more suffering and sadness than one would imagine if one were merely to stick to the proliferation of advertisements and rhetoric about abundance, the good life, the American Dream, window shopping and the melting pot slogan of a land of infinite possibilities and of unity in creative diversity (Mills 1956; Packard 1981[1957]; Marcuse 2002[1964]).[23]

Bernays first put to the test Freud's ideas of subterranean desires and forces lurking beneath the conscious mind of every human being when he was working as a press agent for the American government. During World War I, he served as part of the American war propaganda office, the Committee on Public Information where he used the same persuasive techniques he had used in promoting plays and ballets in helping "win America over to an unpopular war". He was "versed in the hard-nosed tactics needed to capture and keep the attention of the war-weary public in America and abroad" (Tye 1998: 18–19). The communication strategy adopted by him and his fellow propagandists was to show the "importance of ideas as weapons" (Bernays 1961[1923]: xxxii) and to present President Woodrow Wilson's involvement in the war as driven not by the need to restore the power of kings and unelected authorities, but rather, by the need to promote America's principles of freedom and democracy. Wilson was President from 1913 to 1921. Bernays proved to be extremely skilful in promoting these ideas both at home and at work. When the war ended and he accompanied President Wilson to the Paris Peace Conference, the hailing of Wilson as a godhead symbol of liberation further convinced Bernays of his propaganda techniques. He and his colleagues had portrayed Wilson as a liberator and champion of the people, and as the creator of a new world in which the freedom lost to the imperial ambitions of self-centred and greedy rulers could be reclaimed (1961[1923]: xxxii–xxxiii).[24] Bernays had little doubt that the same propaganda used during the war would work in times of peace as well (1961[1923]: xxxii–xxxiii; Bernays 2004[1928]: 28). Convinced of "the potential usefulness of wartime publicity practices in peacetime activities", he created an office in New York and called his activities "Publicity Direction", a term that he eventually replaced with "counsel on public relations" (Bernays 1961[1923]: xxxiii–xxxiv, 2004[1928]: 37, 1947: 115), distancing himself from the word

24

"propaganda", which he believed the Germans had brought into disrepute. As counsel on public relations working with the media and various social groups to bring ideas to the consciousness of the public (Bernays 2004[1928]: 38), Bernays saw his chief function to be analysing "objectively and realistically" the position of his client "vis-à-vis a public and to advise as to the necessary corrections" in his client's "attitudes toward and approaches to that public". He was therefore "an instrument for achieving adjustment if any maladjustment in relationships exists" (Bernays 1947: 116). His first book on the theme and practice of persuasive communication was appropriately, however paradoxically, titled *Propaganda*, by which he was keen to stress a more positive, new, modern usage of the word – "a consistent, enduring effort to create or shape events to influence the relations of the public to an enterprise, idea or group" (Bernays 2004[1928]: 25).[25]

Armed with his newly coined professional title of "counsel on public relations", Bernays set his eyes on exploring mechanisms and a machinery to effectively manage and alter the way in which the rapidly increasing populations of the fast industrialising cities of the US thought and felt about themselves and their world. The writings of his uncle Freud proved to be extremely inspiring in this mission. Bernays was particularly fascinated by Freud's idea of hidden irrational forces inside human beings. His immediate ambition was to make money by manipulating the unconscious.

Bernays was attracted by the idea that more than information and rationality determine human decision making among individuals and groups. He began to invest in understanding the impact of the irrational and emotional selves of people in the decisions they make and in how they act. It was not enough to feed people with facts, because facts were not enough to determine behaviour. Irrespective of claims to the contrary by journalists and scientists, Bernays believed that facts do not speak for themselves; they depend on the individuals and groups whose behaviour they are supposed to influence to take on particular meanings and to be effective. What individuals, acting as individuals or as part of a group, bring to facts are their hidden desires and fears – their submerged emotions – that make facts powerful and effective or without consequence. Put differently, facts need an emotional context to make sense, but emotions do not need facts to ring true.

Just like imperial powers turned to the popular classes for their experimentations (on power and inhibitions and on the inhibitions of power), Bernays turned to the popular classes for his own experiments. As new neoliberal empires would rise and spread globally, the popular classes of America would join the popular classes and so-called tribal or primitive populations of the rest of the world as guinea pigs. Dark individual forces would be complemented by the supposedly dark forces of the primitive and savage zones of the world. Salvation for these peoples would mean overcoming the internalised fear induced by "pre-scientific", "pre-logical" or simply "irrational" traditions – freeing themselves from the inhibitions that come with primitive traditions, and embracing the rational, positivist, scientific discourses of Western modernity (Lerner 1958), often presented in subtle ways, using techniques of *subliminal stimulation* and *subliminal seduction* (Packard 1981[1957) aimed at getting them to states of heightened suggestibility.

Among Bernays's experiments was his persuasion of women, for whom smoking in public was a taboo, to smoke. It was an experiment conducted on behalf of George Washington Hill, President of the American Tobacco Company, who was keen to break the taboo against women smoking in public and even at home.[26] Having successfully promoted cigarettes as "manly things" and "the stuff of warriors" and ensured that "their use among men soared" in the interest of profits, the tobacco companies were "convinced ... that the time was ripe to open a second front, this time targeting females" (Tye 1998:

23). The parallel is remarkable, with subsequent techniques of persuasive communication adopted by advocates of modernisation and/or Westernisation encouraging individuals in other parts of the non-Western world to, in the manner of *les évolués* of French colonial Africa, defy the taboos and beliefs of their cultures and traditions, and become Western through adopting or adapting themselves to consume Western ideas, goods and behaviour (Lerner 1958; Schramm 1964; Kunczik 1993). This makes of European or Western civilisation not really about suppression of barbarities in the metropoles deemed to be rational, but about externalising and outsourcing as much as possible the barbarities and irrationalities of Europe to the peripheries and the purportedly dark recesses of the world. In this sense, colonisation was not merely about suppressing African barbarities but it was also about implanting European barbarities onto the continent, a motivating assumption being that Europeans considered themselves in the metropole to be rational and therefore human, as opposed to the irrational and emotive animals and sub-humans in the colonial peripheries badly in need of a civilising mission (however uncivil and anti-social) that would replace, in principle, belief with science, backwardness with development, autocracy with democracy, the group with the individual, public ownership and control of resources with private ownership, and control and with a market economy.

As part of the experiment to normalise women smoking, Bernays sought the services of a psychoanalyst to find out what cigarettes meant to women.[27] The psychoanalyst told him that cigarettes were a symbol of the penis and of male sexual power, adding that if Bernays could find a way to connect cigarettes with the idea of challenging male power, then women would smoke, as the cigarette would take on the meaning of a substitute male penis, meaning that women could have penises of their own and not have to depend on men who lorded over them. Bernays decided to stage an event at the yearly Easter day parade in New York, which attracted thousands of participants. He agreed with a group of young "suffragettes" (freedom- and equality-seeking women) to hide cigarettes under their clothes and to join the parade, and await his signal for them to light up the cigarettes dramatically. He then mobilised the press to watch out for a group of suffragettes who had planned to attend the parade to protest by lighting up what they called torches of freedom. He had thought things through carefully. He planned to reach out and contain the outcry that was bound to be provoked by the symbolic subversion of male power by presenting the act as a gesture of freedom and a statement on equality between the sexes. The effect was immediate. In New York and across the US and around the world, there was a remarkable rise in the sale of cigarettes to women. Bernays had made smoking by women socially acceptable with a single symbolic act of subversion (Tye 1998: 23-50).[28]

What Bernays had created was the idea that if a woman smoked, it made her more powerful and independent. An idea that led to corporations opening up their smoking rooms to women five weeks after the event, and that persists today.[29] This successfully orchestrated event around women smoking made him realise that it was possible to persuade people to behave irrationally if products were linked to their emotional desires and feelings.[30] The idea that smoking actually made women freer was completely irrational, but it made them feel more independent. It meant that apparently irrelevant objects could become powerful emotional symbols of how one wanted to be seen by others. With this idea he rapidly earned the reputation of a consummate propagandist who could help anyone sell just about anything for a fee by making people feel that their esteem could rise and fall in the eyes of others, depending on the things they had and how they displayed or consumed the things they had (Bernays 1961[1923]; Tye 1998: 23–50).[31]

To Bernays, an effective way of selling a product (be this a consumer item, an idea, the image of a politician or any other public figure) is not only to sell the said product to the intellect of the prospective buyer but, also and even more effectively, to the buyer's feelings. This he did by pushing advertisers to suggest either directly or subliminally that buyers would feel better if they bought the product being advertised. Arguing that people are very often driven by motives and desires which they conceal from themselves, Bernays elaborates on why people may purchase things which they do not really need.

> A thing may be desired not for its intrinsic worth or usefulness, but because he [the consumer] has unconsciously come to see in it a symbol of something else, the desire for which he is ashamed to admit to himself. A man buying a car may think he wants it for purposes of locomotion, whereas the fact may be that he would really prefer not to be burdened with it, and would rather walk for the sake of his health. He may really want it because it is a symbol of social position, an evidence of his success in business, or a means of pleasing his wife (Bernays 2004[1928]: 52).

Similarly, although abandoning one's traditions in favour of the traditions and ways of life of another might make no sense intellectually – or in terms of Cartesian rationalism and its logic of separation between mind and body – the idea that one would feel better and be well regarded by global validators of social status and tastes, was compelling enough for one to want to invest in doing something apparently so irrational as to set aside the cultural values in which one had been socialised and groomed to the point of considering them as natural. It is thus little wonder that the same techniques of persuasive communication employed by Bernays to sell products were adopted and have continued to be used by communication professionals and technicians called upon to propose effective models of social change, modernisation or development in non-Western contexts, which mostly comprise former colonies of Europe. In tune with such expectations of Westernisation posing as modernity, communication professionals generally assume their role to be that of persuading societies and people deemed to be trapped in the darkness of irrational cultures, beliefs and practices to abandon such traditions in favour of more rational alternatives inspired by the enlightened West (America in particular), where they were assumed to be the normal way of life (Lerner 1958; Schramm 1964; Kunczik 1993) and the ultimate validation of what it meant to be human and modern.[32]

In terms of consumer behaviour, Bernays was successful in bringing need and want into conversation, and significantly, giving want, desire and appetite the upper hand. He made currency of the idea that to purchase something was not just because one needed it and had rational justifications for having it, but also, and crucially, that one was engaging oneself emotionally and personally in the product or service. Purchasing then becomes something motivated not just by need but also because the thing purchased makes one feel better. It satisfies not only intellectual or rational needs, but emotional needs as well. Being emotionally connected to a product or service is as significant as actually needing that product or service. Cartesian rationalism was not enough, and rational choices were not always central because consumers were, above all, emotional individuals. It was not enough to think and to behave rationally; feeling was equally, if not more, important. Bernays thus called on big business to "have its finger continuously on the public pulse", and to seek to "understand the changes in the public mind and be prepared to interpret itself fairly and eloquently to changing opinion", motivated more by desire and feeling than by reason and logic (Bernays 2004[1928]: 91).

Bernays had resolved a major problem for American corporations – the danger of overproduction. If people were limited to consuming only that which they had a need for, there was the risk that a point would come when people had enough goods and would simply stop buying. Necessity might be the mother of all inventions, but need and necessity were not enough to keep companies in business, especially in the era of mass production. Functionality and durability alone were dangerous for business, and so was an advertisement industry that was simply confined to showing consumers the practical virtues of a product (Bernays 2004[1928]: 63–91; Packard 1981[1957].[33] Bernays had offered American corporations the opportunity to transform the way the majority of Americans thought about their products and services. His role was to cultivate the new consumer driven by desire and not merely by need. He actively encouraged consumers to desire and to need their wants and want their needs. In his own words, he saw his role as that of "the engineering of consent" (Bernays 1947; The F. W. Faxon Company 1951),[34] an expression that subsequently inspired the related expression of how the media actively propagate the ideas of the economic and political elite in the US and elsewhere by "manufacturing consent" and reducing ordinary citizens into hapless spectators (Herman and Chomsky 1988) in a society of mass-mediated spectacle (Debord 1990).

Bernays elaborated on what he meant by "the engineering of consent", which to him affected almost every aspect of the daily lives of Americans. He described it as "action based only on thorough knowledge of the situation and on the application of scientific principles and tried practices to the task of getting people to support ideas and programs" (Bernays 2004[1928]: 114). It amounted to the freedom to shape public opinion through persuasion and, as such, was "the very essence of the democratic process" (Bernays 2004[1928]: 114). Successful engineering of consent depended on "the complete understanding of those whom it attempts to win over" (Bernays 2004[1928]: 114). However, because leaders were often confronted with pressing crises and the urgent need to make decisions, they had to reckon with the fact that they might increasingly have to outsource the putting together of the requisite understanding to "the educational processes, as well as other available techniques" (Bernays 2004[1928]: 114) provided by the crystallising profession of counsels of public relations, in order to avoid "time lags, blind spots, and points of weakness" in decision making and expedient action (Bernays 2004[1928]: 115). While some of Bernays's contemporaries like Friedrick Hayek were largely supportive of the engineering, manufacturing or orchestration of spontaneity and consent in the interest of the affluent consumer society,[35] others like John Kenneth Galbraith questioned the dependency culture of such apparently affluent societies that championed consumer sovereignty in principle brought about by making people desire products that they really did not need (Williams 2001).

Bernays's investment in mining the irrational for profit knew no bounds. He developed the practice of linking products to famous Hollywood film stars and celebrities and introduced the practice of product placement in the movies. He would dress the stars at the film's premiere with clothes and jewellery from firms that he represented. He encouraged car companies to sell cars as symbols of male sexuality, and with this would come a whole new dimension of sexual suggestiveness in the body, build and presentation of different models of cars. He and his fellow practitioners of public relations, advertising and marketing are largely to be credited with the colonisation, commodification and commercialisation of every single orifice and morsel of the human body by commercial interests determined to spread consumerism with evangelical zeal.[36] The more Bernays succeeded the more manipulative and economical with the truth he became. He would employ psychologists to issue reports that lauded the quality of products for the consumer and then pretend to pass those reports for independent studies. He readily came to the rescue of corporations that had miscalculated by mass producing a product (cigarettes for example) with the wrong packet colour (green in one instance), by presenting the mistake to consumers as innovative, pacesetting and trendy – the best packaging ever imagined. In other words, he did not hesitate to sacrifice the truth for falsehood if this would help him sell products in spite of the ethical obligations and responsibilities of the profession he founded. As he argued, it was unthinkable to "accept public relations as a profession", without equally expecting it "to have both ideals and ethics" (2004[1928]: 44). Like the ambitious John Moray of the costume drama series *The Paradise* – a 2012 BBC television adaptation of Émile Zola's novel *Au Bonheur des Dames* (*The Ladies' Paradise*) (2008[1883]) – Bernays would organise fashion shows in department stores and pay celebrities to repeat the new and essential message that appetite and desire were supreme indicators of one's true character. Consumers were encouraged to get used to the idea that they bought things not just for need but to express their inner sense of self to others. Hidden psychological factors determine what a person consumes and desires to consume, and it behoves the astute consumer to listen to that inner voice calling out for him/her to get his/her consumer instincts right (Bernays 1961[1923], 2004[1928], 1947, 1952; The F. W. Faxon Company 1951; Tye 1998).[37]

Of Bernays, Larry Tye has observed that not only did he refuse to be constrained by convention he consciously defied convention, convinced as he was that ordinary rules did not apply to him and that he could reshape reality (Tye 1998: 52). Bernays contributed significantly to transforming America from a culture of needs to a culture of desires. He pointed American corporations and subsequently political elite in the direction of how to school ordinary Americans to desire, to want and to cultivate an appetite for new things without having to bother whether or not the old things have been entirely consumed or used up. Prosperity for corporations depended on the extent to which they were able to make desire overshadow need in the American and global consumers they targeted with their mass-produced products. If Americans have since the 1920s tended to consider their importance to their country much more in terms of the extent to which they are consumers than through the referent of being legal and political citizens, it is largely thanks to Bernays's creative, albeit contentious, application of Freud's ideas. It is also to his credit that the American economy and increasingly economies the world over are more commonly described as a consumer economy, where desire is more relevant than need, and consumer citizenship seemingly more valued than political citizenship. Even culture is understood more as consumer culture, than merely in its general sense (Marcuse 2002[1964]; Goodwin et al. 1997; Chomsky 1999; Featherstone 2007). Outsourcing reason and cultural production to hidden persuaders at the service of dubious ambitions of the corporate and political elite has reduced citizens to passive consumers of options instead of actively participating in the creative imagination and production of the things and values they are schooled to hold dear. *"I consume therefore I am"*[38] has come to carry more weight than René Descartes's famous *"Cogito ergo sum"* (*"I think therefore I am"*) (Descartes 2003[1637]).

4

The Rational Consumer:
Bad for Business and Politics

In January 2018, my wife and daughter returned from a holiday in Cambodia with a T-shirt with an inscription that caught my attention: "*Same Same but Different*". The inscription speaks to Bernays's idea of the similarities between big business and politics. They can both be administered the same drug or conned by the same consummate conman or dealmaker, despite their apparent differences as patients or clients. Both are preoccupied with the headache of how to control the savage dangerous enemy forces within. Bernays had proven in his dealings with American corporations that such irrational forces could be managed and mastered. He was constantly hunting for opportunities to take his techniques of persuasive communication beyond his public relations work for America's big business. When the leadership of America's political establishment came knocking, Bernays served them exactly the same dish that he had perfected for America's corporate elite (Tye 1998: 77–90). As Larry Tye puts it, "If housewives could be guided in their selection of soap", and "husbands in their choice of a car", so too could "voters in their selection of candidates. And candidates in their political posturing. Indeed, the very substance of American thought was mere clay to be molded by the savvy public relations practitioner, or so it seemed" (Tye 1998: viii). Why change a winning formula? Bernays was convinced he "could change not only the way people bought but the way they thought" (Tye 1998: x). If the rational consumer is bad for business, why should the rational voter or politician be any different for politics? If the masses cannot be trusted with making rational decisions on what and what not to consume, why should they be entrusted with making rational decisions on state policies and the future direction of American society? His inspired experience of the world and the way things worked had reduced him to a workman whose only tool was a hammer and to whom every problem was a nail. Using his hammer of dangerous forces that made it impossible for the ordinary populace and masses to be rational, however hard they tried, he extended his relevance into the realm of politics (Bernays 2004[1928]: 92–114).

Bernays's first opportunity to test his ideas in politics came with President John Calvin Coolidge in 1924. Republican and President from 1920 to 1928, Coolidge was a taciturn man by nature. He had become a national joke. In a bid to change his image, he was pointed in the direction of Bernays, who had proven his worth as a public relations genius with American corporations. Bernays's solution was to employ the same salesmanship that he had employed to help corporations sell products (Tye 1998: 77–79). As the engineer of consent that he was, Bernays operated on the basis that he had to create news, if he wanted to shape the attitudes and actions of the American people towards their president. It was his conviction that: "Newsworthy events, involving people, usually do not happen by accident. They are planned deliberately to accomplish a purpose, to influence our ideas and actions." (Bernays 1947: 119).[39] The reasoning was simple: if you can sell a thing, you can sell a person. Or, as he put it, "Good government can be sold to a community just as any other commodity can be sold." (Bernays 2004[1928]: 105). Additionally, Bernays drew inspiration from the words of President Wilson, a foremost proponent of publicity, whose words on the subject he quoted in the preface to the new edition of *Crystalizing Public Opinion*. In his presidential campaign in 1912, Wilson reportedly affirmed that:

... publicity is one of the purifying elements of politics. The best thing that you can do with anything that is crooked is to lift it up where people can see that it is crooked, and then it will either straighten itself out or disappear. Nothing shakes all the bad practices of politics like exposure (Woodrow Wilson cited in Bernays 1961[1923]: xxxii).

It was thus necessary, Bernays concluded, to maintain the freedom of the media, information and communication technologies, and kindred weapons of publicity used to shape and influence public opinion (1961[1923]: xl).

Bernays's strategy was to cleanse President Coolidge's public image by arranging for thirty famous film stars to visit the White House, meet and spend time with the President. Having already succeeded in using his public relations skills to assist big business in manipulating not just the feelings and desires of consumers, but also the press with the stories they package and place in various media outlets in the form of advertisements, Bernays mobilised the press for maximum coverage of the staged White House event. What could be more newsworthy than bringing Hollywood celebrities to meet the celebrity of politics (even one that was a national joke) in the White House? When the next day Bernays discovered, to his greatest satisfaction, that the visit was featured as front page coverage in every newspaper in the United States, he knew instantly that he had succeeded in linking politics with public relations and the cultural (mass media, film and entertainment, celebrities, etc.) industries (Bernays 2004[1928]: 102; Tye 1998: 77–79).[40] Thenceforth, politics would be incomplete without a public relations component, and politicians would soon understand the value of seeking to harness or manipulate the unconscious desires of the voting public and aggressive forces, especially when dealing with crowds, such as those often mobilised by politicians to attend political rallies (Herman and Chomsky 1988; Chomsky 1989, 1999, 2002, 2004; Barsamian

1994a, 1994b; Tye 1998; Brock 2005; Nichols and McChesney 2013; Sherman 2017; Marcotte 2018). As more and more political leaders subscribed to his spin (Tye 1998: 77–90), Bernays perfected his recipe, a central component of which became the importance of language in political discourse:

> ... he knew how much more appealing an active candidate was than a passive one. So he made a list of verbs that should guide the campaign's actions: express (confidence), assail, deny, predict, hail, ask, promise, appeal, urge, hope, advocate, see, say, tell, declare, deplore, request, remark, reveal, propose, condemn, exhort, praise, forecast, demand, thank (Tye 1998: 82).

To Bernays, not only was "The conscious and intelligent manipulation of the organized habits and opinions of the masses ... an important element in democratic society", those who did the manipulation "constitute an invisible government which is the true ruling power" of a democratic society such as America (Bernays 2004[1928]: 9). He saw propaganda or public relations practised by "shrewd persons operating behind the scenes" (Bernays 2004[1928]: 35) as "the executive arm of the invisible government" – those who moulded minds, formed tastes and suggested ideas that governed attitudes, practices and choices, thereby contributing significantly in organising the chaos that was modern life – in the interest of America's corporate and political elite (Bernays 2004[1928]: 20).

Now that he had brought big business and politics into conversation in awareness of the dangerous attractions of the unconscious aggressions lurking beneath the purportedly rational self, Bernays used his powerful imagination to help big business create a vision of the utopia that free market capitalism would bring about in American society and globally eventually, if given the opportunity to prove itself. He sought to link democracy and American business. He wanted to equate capitalism with democracy and democracy with

38

capitalism, and literally, he manipulated people to think that real democracy was only possible in a capitalist society, just as real capitalism had to be associated only with a proclaimed democratic society. To him, democracy and capitalism was a match made in heaven; both understood the importance of keeping up the appearance of being deeply rooted in principles of rational choice, while in reality actively manipulating the irrational forces in consumers and voters by feeding palliatives of happiness and docility to them in the interest of market and political stability. One only needs to look at the highly psychologistic undertones of social scientific writings coming out of the USA and American-educated scholars of other nationalities to fathom the extent to which Bernays's ideas captured America's imagination. It must be said, however, that his was a form of democracy that depended on treating people not as active citizens but as passive consumers of products and political fodder eagerly brought their way by the economic and political elite. In Bernays's democracy, it is not the people but their desires that are in charge. People are reduced to unthinking consumers driven by instinctual unconscious desires easily triggered by carefully choreographed subliminal messages prepared and delivered on behalf of the economic and political elite by the public relations firms and professionals they hire to promote what they want – more of the same (Bernays 2004[1928], 1947; Mills 1956; Packard 1981[1957]; Marcuse 2002[1964]; Goodwin et al. 1997; Chomsky 1999; Tye 1998; Featherstone 2007).

Like his uncle Freud, Bernays appreciated the virtues of freedom and democracy in principle. And like Freud, he was concerned that the unconscious forces and irrational violent drives in individuals and crowds could very easily be manipulated or exploited by opportunistic politicians, fundamentalists and exclusionary claims of identity and belonging, with devastating consequences. If uncontained, these forces could easily break through and overwhelm democracy and its market logic. The fears and related emotions of the public could be whipped up to harvest votes rightly or wrongly for a demagogue, a populist, a charlatan or a conman, and for dubious or contested causes (e.g. Trump's tsunami of populism and narrow nationalism in an age of globalisation and cosmopolitanism; or to question, precipitously, the established order of things and the very nature of a given society (McCain 2018)).[41] Such would be the case, for example, of a leader who enjoys extraordinary outpouring of mass adulation, but who at the same time indulges in and encourages the systematic manipulation of emotions by whipping up and unleashing mass hatred against the purported enemies (within and without) of their society (narrowly defined in rigidly exclusionary terms) or those defined as not quite belonging. It could also be done by a leader of tenuous legitimacy, who comes to power via means of Electoral College votes despite losing the popular vote, aided and abetted by carefully gerrymandered redistricting motivated by invidious partisan intent (Raymond with Spiegelman 2008). To Bernays, responsible leadership entailed constant awareness of the possibility of the use of the engineering of consent to subvert the status quo, public values and the public interest, while the counsel on public relations on the other hand had "a professional responsibility to push only those ideas he can respect, and not to promote causes or accept assignments for clients he considers antisocial" (Bernays 1947: 115–116).

It is curious to read Bernays's writings after the 2016 presidential election in the USA. This was an election which Donald J. Trump won (surprisingly to some, though not to others who have kept a keen eye on the ever surging role played by advertising and public relations in American politics). Trump is a renowned estate agent and an outstanding student of Bernays in terms of his salesmanship and flare for propaganda and manipulation of the media and public opinion (Trump with Schwartz 1987; Ross with McLean 2005; Trump with McIver and Kiyosaki with Lechter 2006; Trump with

McIver 2007, 2008; Johnston 2016). As addicted to the media as was Bernays, Trump has excelled at persuasive techniques developed by Bernays, ranging from what he has termed "truthful hyperbole" (Trump with Schwartz 1987: 58)[42] to trolling (Marcotte 2018) and semantic infiltration, through the relentless attack, denial, distancing, discrediting, delegitimation, deflection and diversion of others, from political opponents to the media and beyond.[43] He is also a long term Democrat recently turned Republican to ease his political aspirations and populist nationalism. During the election, he was considered by some as a candidate with unique vulnerabilities and liabilities and as a man widely believed to have perfected the art of the con ("Conman Don" some call him) (O'Brien 2016[2007]; Johnston 2016),[44] aided and abetted perhaps, by what George Will has characterised as his being "syntactically challenged".[45] Described as a person with no ideology, no principles, no morals, no scruples and no convictions, Trump is likened to a flip-flopping lone tree that leans every way the wind blows. This is said to make of him an imperfect vessel for a bigger right wing movement, someone who ticks all the boxes on how to cover political mileage through mobilisation and weaponisation of the very worst in being human. During his campaign, he embraced, whipped up and made political capital of public sentiments and practices such as being fearful, angry and hateful, bearing grudges and being self-absorbed, having little regard for the truth and for the history of mobility that made it possible for him to be where he is today – America – as a white American of European descent. He is seen as notorious for burning bridges and building walls with nonstop radioactive rhetoric of negativity, divisiveness and exclusionism – what comedian Jon Stewart has termed "gleeful cruelty", "gratuitous dickishness" and "Dickensian level of villainy".[46] Trump triumphed not only by making political capital of the unconscious desires of fear, anger and hate in his voters, but also by harnessing social media, Twitter in particular,[47] to whip up the mass production and distribution of energising fear, hatred, paranoia, propaganda and conspiracy theories with the assistance of conservative Republican media outlets such as Fox News, Fox & Friends, Sinclair Broadcast Group and Breitbart (Brock 2005; Sherman 2017). He has revived and revamped these conservative media outlets (Marcotte 2018) to serve as "mere destructive propaganda machines" or "Trump Spin Machines",[48] not dissimilar to state-owned, government-controlled media in a dictatorship and totalitarian context (Nyamnjoh 2005; Klaas 2017).[49] According to *The New York Times*, Trump was reportedly displeased when on "a recent trip overseas, Melania Trump's television aboard Air Force One was tuned to CNN... He raged at his staff for violating a rule that the White House entourage should begin each trip tuned to Fox — his preferred network over what he considers the 'fake news' CNN".[50] He used Twitter effectively to insert himself into and redirect in his favour public conversations and debates, causing many a controversy (*The Daily Show* with Noah and Meacham 2018).[51] He relied on his lieutenants like campaign manager, Steve Bannon, and his son-in-law, Jared Kushner, who in turn relied on what Cambridge Analytica fed them by Julius Assange of WikiLeaks[52] and from its very own repertoire of psychological and lifestyle profiling of 87 million Facebook-using Americans,[53] to successfully run a campaign in which truth, thoughtfulness, reasonableness, logic and constancy and consistency of imagination and articulation played little or no part (Johnston 2016; Green 2017; Koffler 2017; Clapper with Brown 2018; Comey 2018; Frum 2018; Hayden 2018; Isikoff and Corn 2018; Lewandowski and Bossie 2018; Nance 2018; Spicer 2018; Watts 2018; Wolff 2018).[54]

In the mainstream liberal media and critical publications on the other hand, Trump was widely presented as a pathological or congenital liar – someone constitutionally incapable of telling the truth and a champion of many a conspiracy theory of right wing populism – who projected his lies onto others, accused everyone else but himself of lying, and seldom apologised for anything, not even when literally caught with his pants down (Spicer 2018).[55] He reportedly behaved more like a king who is always right (even in his swimming trunks), than as someone supposedly sensitive to the idea of rule of law as championed by American liberal democracy. He was said to delight in gaslighting and in intentionally bewildering people with claims that were just not true (Carpenter 2018). As Amanda Carpenter explains, Trump has perfected the art of gaslighting, a tactic of political manipulation and influencing public opinion that she traces back to President Richard Nixon:

> First, he stakes out political territory no one else would dare occupy, taking over the news cycle. Next, he denies responsibility while simultaneously advancing the story. His third step may be his most maddening: he creates suspense for his story by saying more information is coming soon. His fourth step is carefully selecting a detractor to attack, often finding the weakest opponent or someone who will be severely damaged by taking a roll in the mud with him. If he's successful, and sometimes even when he's not, he'll proceed to the fifth step: declaring victory under any circumstance. (Carpenter 2018: back cover).

Often appearing unhinged and unglued, obsessive, profoundly reckless and determined to respond to taunts with taunts, Trump quarrelled with all those who sought to remind him of any rules of the game that required finesse, respect and recognition of the dignity, rights and entitlements of all and sundry among American nationals and citizens, as well as the country's varying categories of admirers, visitors and guests. Not only was absolute regressive republican white tribalism his instinctive first port of call, he seemed patient with democracy only to the extent that he was victorious, even if this took corrupting the rules of the game by putting in place his own referees to ensure the game was played in his favour.[56] Inclusivity and cosmopolitanism as the fruit of a world on the move were not part of his rhetoric and campaign slogans of "America First" and "Make America Great Again", as he left few in doubt that his America was one increasingly without a sense of history and on a crusade of purity and purification that had little sympathy for anyone who was not unapologetically and supremely white and autochthonous, even if not autochthonous enough to claim the status of Native-American (Wong 2010). At the bottom rungs of his ever-diminishing circles of whiteness and indicators of Americanness, he located Africans and Latinos,[57] the ultimate revulsions around which he built his build-a-wall anti-immigrant campaign for the office of President. All manner of crimes and afflictions are fabricated and projected onto these purportedly reckless sweat-footed "barbarians" or "animals"[58] who keep knocking at the doors of the civilisation that the purity of whiteness and its unfathomable genius have made possible in Europe and the United States of America.[59] He may pose as a non-elitist anti-establishment populist and be hailed as champion of those Hilary Clinton regrettably referred to during the 2016 presidential campaign as "deplorables"[60] – among whom are millions of American nationals who genuinely fall through the cracks of the material fulfilment of citizenship and *The American Dream* despite the drudgery and sacrifices of toiling to make a decent living (Bruder 2017) –, but he is all too eager to use children (including babies and toddlers) as pawns and hostages by separating them from parents whom he in his zero-tolerance immigration policy perceives as "the untouchables" fleeing persecution and knocking for accommodation and compassion at the American border with Mexico.[61] He insists that 'the United States will not be a migrant camp and it will not be a refugee holding facility' under his watch.[62] And to prove his determination, however morally abominable, and despite the public outcry of Americans protesting his "government-sanctioned child abuse" around the rallying call of "this is not who we are",[63] the babies, toddlers and children are imprisoned, jailed or interned in child internment camps which his enthusiastic lieutenants have euphemistically named "Tender Age Shelters".[64] Even after the public national and international outrage and condemnation compelled Trump to reluctantly cave to the moral conscience of the nation and humanity, by signing an executive order reversing the policy of keeping detained children away from their detained parents, he still insisted that the over 2,300 children already separated from their parents would not be reunited with their families.[65] The public outrage around the controversial policy earned Trump an unenviable spot on the cover of *Time* magazine depicting him towering over a sobbing immigrant Honduran toddler, along with the sarcastic words "Welcome to America".[66] As a divisive master of divide-and-rule, he wanted and succeeded in making Americans increasingly uncertain, unsure and in perpetual conflict with one another (Johnston 2016; Clapper with Brown 2018; Comey 2018; Dionne Jr. et al. 2017; Frum 2018; Hayden 2018; Isikoff and Corn 2018; Nance 2018; Watts 2018; Wolff 2018).[67]

Granted Trump's reported egomaniac congenital insensitivity to the pain of others, how could Americans across the melting-pot spectrum of their country have expected to make a caring leader of an uncaring salesman? Powerful as the media are usually considered to be, Trump succeeded significantly in rendering them impotent by appealing narrowly to a credulous core base of Republican voters and by repeatedly referring to critical journalists as "the enemy of the people".[68] The "corrupt" or "fake" mainstream media, as he and his supporters love to call media practitioners critical of him, are repeatedly accused by Trump of trafficking in fake news, hoaxes and witch hunts, merely because their favourite candidate, Hillary Clinton, lost the 2016 presidential election to him (Jarrett 2018; Pirro 2018).[69] They, in turn, tend to represent him as stunningly superficial, hollow, ignorant, ill-informed, incurious, insecure, paranoid, hypersensitive, impetuous, impulsive,[70] erratic, reckless, domineering, megalomaniac, childish,[71] immature, easily distracted, narcissistic, delusional, conscienceless, lacking in moral integrity, unethical and untethered to the truth, valueless and insensitive to every shred of human decency and honour. As some of his critics would say, Trump is capable of standing perfectly in the rain and claiming it was a sunny day (Johnston 2016; Clapper with Brown 2018; Comey 2018; Frum 2018; Dionne Jr. et al. 2017; Hayden 2018; Isikoff and Corn 2018; Marcotte 2018; Wolff 2018). The cacophony of Trump's addiction to forgetfulness and compulsion to lying in the interest of divisiveness has deafened him to "what truth sounds like" (Dyson 2018) and to the capacity which past presidents and leaders have developed to look forward rather than back and to assert hope over fear in forging the core values that have come to constitute "the soul of America" (Meacham 2018). To the over 60 per cent of Americans (if regular polls are to be believed) critical of Trump and his rhetoric Bernays's assertion that: "Propaganda is of no use to the politician unless he has something to say which the public, consciously or unconsciously, wants to hear" (Bernays 2004[1928]: 109) would make perfect sense.

Trump's supporters are suspicious of the mainstream "corrupt" or "fake media" and follow pro-Trump conservative news outlets religiously and dutifully (Spicer 2018; Jarrett 2018; Pirro 2018). As Sarah Palin would put it, they wear the scorn of the liberal media with pride.[72] Together, Trump and the conservative media, by sheer persistence and the art of repeatedly sticking to stating and restating untruths and/or being economical with the facts of a given issue, are able to keep his support and base trustful while ignoring everyone else (Spicer 2018; Jarret 2018; Pirro 2018). Despite being criticised of having no proven track record with veracity and of ad nauseam corrosive lying and distortion of the truth, Trump has proven himself a public relations and propaganda genius through his capacity to deafly state and restate lie after lie, knowing that, ultimately, the truth would stand little chance with his lies, especially with public opinion among his staunch supporters and Republican base. Some observers would argue that the uncritical endorsement displayed by Trump supporters borders on religious fervour (Marcotte 2018). Trump's successful salesmanship in packaging and marketing himself to Republicans as a messianic populist, means that to his base whatever he says or does is right. No amount of evidence, no wrongdoing seems able to shake their faith in Trump as saviour and bearer of salvation. If perception is reality, who needs facts (Lewandowski and Bossie 2018; Spicer 2018; Jarrett 2018; Pirro 2018)? As Bernays would have put it, Trump has perfected the art of engineering consent with "words [that] hammer continually at the eyes and ears of America", magnifying thousands of times his carefully choreographed self-serving narratives and accounts of events (Bernays 1947: 113). He and his echo chambers are said to readily take credit for success but not the blame for failure. If his followers so readily believe his deliberate falsehoods, outlandish lies and bending the truth to suit his own narratives, even to the point of falling off the cliff of insanity,[73] what would push him to take facts and the truth seriously?[74] But then, what is the purpose of power without a moral compass, especially in a capitalist society that some would wish and insist should continue to take seriously its real or assumed democratic credentials and on passing for *the* global gendarme of good democratic governance? How much bigotry would it take to undo the glue of American democracy as a capitalist society where patriotism has come to mean a multiplicity of shoppers of diverse backgrounds shopping from a sumptuous menu of creative diversity[75] (Johnston 2016; Clapper with Brown 2018;

Comey 2018; Frum 2018; Hayden 2018; Isikoff and Corn 2018; Marcotte 2018; Wolff 2018)?

Naively or not, Bernays thought outcomes such as Trump could be avoided, by providing for a rational elite united around a common set of values and propped up by hidden persuaders like himself,[76] as "tamers of the wild crowd and guardians of a civil society" (Tye 1998: 92). Could his effusive optimism be understood in these terms? His tendency to view:

> ... activities with which he was involved in epic terms, as events that helped shape American and world culture ... . He was exceedingly proprietary about his role in those events, seeing himself as having battled for the public good as others succumbed to temptation, and doing all he could to ensure that history would see him in the same heroic light. And he always got the last word because he outlived contemporaries ... (Tye 1998: 20).

Notwithstanding the fact that he lived for 103 years, Bernays did not live long enough to blame himself for having pushed too far his adoption and adaptation of his uncle's ideas and ideals. In his estimation, the sort of political opportunism and demagoguery that delivers the likes of Trump could be contained if the masses were guided to vote correctly, and to make the right choices. Protecting stability and the status quo was a superior duty and responsibility to unleashing the impulsive forces of change in directions that one could not predict or control. The fact that people have unconscious fears and unrecognised longings is enough reason to worry that if not closely guided, some opportunist could tap into the deepest desires and deepest fears of the public and use these to foster the ends, designs and purposes of such an opportunist – ends, designs and purposes that were not necessarily compatible with the overarching and cherished values and visions of established society. In Trump's case, it would appear, if his critics are right, that he is driven by delusions of grandeur, greedy overindulgence, expectations of blind loyalty[77], narcissistic autocratic cravings worthy of a banana republic[78] and a truly instinctual, primitive, stunted, rudimentary form of being human, trapped in the depths of the irrational (Clapper with Brown 2018; Comey 2018; Hayden 2018; Klaas 2017; Marcotte 2018; Wolff 2018). In the manner of autocrats and monarchs, he seems to crave exemption from the burdens of ordinary citizenship. These attributes have led *New York Times* columnist Thomas Friedman to conclude that Donald Trump is "The biggest threat to the integrity of … [American] democracy today"[79]. A sentiment echoed by Lili Loofbourow in an op-ed: "The America We Thought We Knew Is Gone" – destroyed by Trump, who has faced no consequences for "his decision to say outrageous, incorrect, inflammatory things", whose "lies meet with no institutional resistance", and who, in consequence, has been rendered "immune to every standard we, as a country, once shared".[80]

To mitigate the materialisation of such autocratic and narcissistic propensities, Bernays encouraged a partnership between the economic and the political elite who knew best what was good for society, and who could – with the assistance of psychologists and public relations experts – connect with the unconscious desires and fears of the masses, weaponise and manipulate them in the interest of the society and social order for which they were responsible. To Bernays, it was pointless and fruitless to use rational arguments or appeal to the reasoning faculties of individual citizens and consumers. He saw groups as malleable and lacking in reliable judgement. Their fears, anxieties and concerns were there to be penetrated, harvested and harnessed by those who knew best – the political and economic elite who oversaw the workings of society. In view of their whimsical and capricious nature, the public could very easily vote for the wrong person or want the wrong thing. Hence the need for "the intelligent minority" to "regiment and guide the masses" from above and with the expertise of hidden persuaders (influential men and women in the shadows) like himself (Bernays 2004[1928]: 114),[81] adept at using subliminal and seductive messaging to advertise and engineer consent (Packard 1981[1957]; Lakhani 2008).[82]

Guiding the voting public and the masses in general involved sharing facts, but also creating facts and indulging in outright disinformation and misinformation campaigns, if need be. Spreading fake news or proliferating tidal waves of lies is a key option on the menu (Bernays 1961[1923], 2004[1928], 1947, 1952; The F. W. Faxon Company 1951; Tye 1998), given that in the field of advertising and public relations, and increasingly in social media as well, if one can repeat something ad infinitum, one can make it credible. Fake news and advertising do not appeal because they are sham or make-believe, they appeal because they purport to be true. An MIT study of "some 126,000 stories, tweeted by 3 million users, over more than 10 years" suggests that truth finds it difficult to compete with hoax and rumour, and that falsehood is more likely to penetrate the Twitter social network further, faster, and deeper than accurate information.[83] This means that even when people on Facebook and Twitter are not confined to "echo chambers" and "filter bubbles", as a study of the browsing histories of 50,000 users based in the US suggests,[84] the risk that they will be exposed less to the truth and more to hoaxes and rumours is not diminished. In his assessment of the 2016 US election and its aftermath, James Clapper, the former Director of National Intelligence under President Obama, concludes that the use of such hoaxes, rumours and fake news promoted by Russia through cyber theft and cyber espionage and Russian advertisement money targeted at the American electorate impacted negatively on the circulation of the truth and swung the election to a Trump win (Clapper with Brown 2018). In Bernays's terms, Vladimir Putin's Russia had launched a successful propaganda war against the USA by manipulating information to sway American public opinion, using the latest enablers and fantasy spaces – social media –, with the passive or active collaboration of the Trump campaign (Brazile 2017; Clinton 2017; Harding 2017; Snyder 2018; Sanger 2018; Watts 2018).[85] In David Corn's view, such collaboration was nothing short of a scandalous betrayal of the USA to a foreign adversary. As he puts it:

> In 2016, Vladimir Putin's regime mounted information warfare against the United States, in part to help Trump become president. While this attack was underway, the Trump crew tried to collude covertly with Moscow, sought to set up a secret communications channel with Putin's office, and repeatedly denied in public that this assault was happening, providing cover to the Russian operation. Trump and his lieutenants aligned themselves with and assisted a foreign adversary, as it was attacking the United States. The evidence is rock-solid: They committed a profound act of betrayal. That is the scandal.[86]

Repeated denials of meddling notwithstanding (Jarrett 2018; Pirro 2018),[87] this is how Vladimir Putin responded to a question on the matter at the press conference following his July 2018 Helsinki summit with Trump. Reuters reporter Jeff Mason asked: "President Putin, did you want President Trump to win the election and did you direct any of your officials to help him do that?" Putin replied: "Yes, I did. Yes, I did. Because he talked about bringing the U.S.–Russia relationship back to normal."[88] Curiously though, while the official transcript of the press conference by the White House seriously edited Mason's question and Putin's response, the official transcript of the Kremlin completely omitted the question and the response, both giving the impression of a calculated attempt to doctor and manipulate what was actually said at the press conference, *à la* Bernays, to achieve the disinformation and misinformation ends desired by both presidents.[89]

Back to Bernays, whose reaction to what he had helped bring about, one can only guess. When American politicians turned to him for help in times of crisis, including during the Cold War, Bernays shared the belief, which was common at the time, that the interests of business and the interests of America were indivisible, especially when faced with the threat of communism. He would use communism, deliberately, as an external enemy, an ideology that had little to do with the core founding values of American society, and therefore as a threat to the American way of life. However, he was convinced that to explain this rationally to the American people was impossible because they were not rational. Instead, he had to devise mechanisms to access their inner fears and manipulate them in the interest of a higher truth.[90] He preferred to engineer or manufacture consent, with the understanding that "people want to go where they want to be led".[91] In his estimation, the truly powerful people were neither the politicians nor the individual voters, but the psychoanalysts and the public relations professionals who had developed ways of reading the public mind and manipulating it to want products and act in tune with messages that numbed them with expectations of stability and the imperative of maintaining the status quo (Bernays 1947).

Through Bernays and with the added and tireless support of his uncle's youngest daughter Anna Freud, with whom "he cemented his relationship as adviser and friend" when he visited her in Vienna in 1949 and eight months later on her first visit to America (Tye 1998: 196–197), psychologists (psychiatrists and psychoanalysts in the main) insinuated themselves into the corridors of power and decision making in American society, and with it came riches, prominence and influence. They continued with Bernays's winning formula. Their message to the political elite was one and the same: The masses were essentially an irrational bunch governed by savage, barbaric dangerous enemy forces lurking just under the surface of normalised society, and therefore not a reliable partner in the business of making rational decisions, and in determining right and wrong, good and bad, insider and outsider, us and them. They were particularly keen on controlling repressed childhood memories of violent feelings and desires, which insinuated irrational and instinctual behaviour into the public arena where rational behaviour was the norm. The capricious nature of these dangerous forces made them particularly unpredictable, as they could be triggered without warning. Needed were human beings that could internalise democratic values enough to withstand the storm of dangerous subterranean forces. To do this effectively involved strengthening the mind to enable it control the inner self better against adversity and insufficiency, and against being overburdened by frustration. It was also to make people feel less helpless and desperate for love. Just as they had successfully created the model consumer, the psychoanalysts doubtlessly believed they could groom the model citizen through their programmes of domestication of the steaming, raw and unpredictable emotions of the American public.[92]

In the esteemed opinion of the Freudian psychoanalysts led by Anna Freud and with Bernays's support in public relations, ensuring rationality, morality and ethics – virtues in short supply – were the exclusive business of the ruling elite – the supposedly "intelligent minorities which need to make use of propaganda continuously and systematically" (Bernays 2004[1928]: 31). It was incumbent on the elite to cultivate a culture that championed these values, and to actively police the behaviour of the unruly masses in order not to jeopardise them. Blind trust in the masses and in public opinion was dangerous. It was their conviction that free market democracy could only work if psychological techniques were used to control the irrationalities of the masses. Democracy was not possible without a ruling elite that was in charge and that could discipline individual citizens at the mercy of irrationality and basic instincts. To create the necessary conditions for the production of individuals capable of behaving as good consumers and as democratic citizens, it was necessary to have the power and economic elite firmly in charge. The psychoanalysts doubling as public relations professionals were very paternalistic both in their view of ordinary people, the voting public and democracy. It is curious to note that what might appear like downright paternalism and a clear contradiction to the basic principles of democracy, did not strike the pro-Freudian psychoanalysts as such. They did not see themselves as working to undermine democracy and the capacities of individual citizens for informed consent. On the contrary, they actually equated what they were engineering as creating the conditions for the future survival of democracy (Stewart-Steinberg 2011).[93]

Within the context of the Cold War, university departments of psychology became popular destinations for millions of dollars in state funds to conduct research on how to alter and control the inner drives of human beings. The psychologists involved in this research not only took for granted that human beings were tussling with dangerous forces hidden beneath their conscious selves, forces that threatened the established social order, but also, they believed that these forces could be controlled, and better still, actually removed from the afflicted persons. Some psychologists sought to have psychiatry in government, influencing politics and politicians, and monitoring political activities because they knew in a rational scientific way what was good for people.[94] Some employed techniques to try and change the fundamental function of individuals to alter their past memories, their past ways of behaving and even to erase everything from their past so that they could restart their lives on a clean slate. This was akin to treating human beings like computers, whose hard disks could be formatted and reformatted to suit the purpose of each individual user. While the politicians were led to believe that they were creating a new and better form of democracy, one that truly responded to the inner feelings of the populace, the aim of the experimenting psychoanalysts was not so much to liberate the people but to develop new ways of controlling them as a means of coping with, neutralising or pre-empting the imponderables of mass democracy. Seldom did they appear to bother about the truism that the past is hardly ever in the past, let alone ever dead.[95]

In this connection, Anna Freud came up with a simple theory of how to control the inner drives. It invited parents and schools, among other public institutions, to teach children how to conform to the rules of society. This was not just because she believed that morality and ethics were important for any society to cohere. She also believed that conforming or properly adjusting to the accepted norms and codes of conduct of their communities and the wider society contributed significantly to keeping the dangerous hidden forces of the unconscious mind in check. It was essential for school children to understand and act upon the fact that uncontrolled emotions brought about uncontrolled actions that affected both the individual child and other children and people around them. Children who conformed were more likely to be successful in containing such forces than those who did not conform. Put differently, harkening to the diktats of established order was the master key to taming the forces of darkness in individuals and, by extension, in the society as a whole. Eventually, the more people perfected their conformity to the accepted patterns of family and social life, the more their self-confidence grew, and the greater their control of the dangerous forces they harboured within themselves (Stewart-Steinberg 2011).[96]

However problematic these prescriptions might seem when examined through the prism of human dignity and freedom of expression, psychoanalysts were somehow convinced that their thinking and practice could bring about a better society. If they could change or reconfigure the way the mind functioned, capturing, caging or permanently deleting/erasing the violent and hurtful dimensions of the human mind and the human being by extension, then this could bring about a truly happy, hopeful, peaceful and accommodating society for all and sundry. Happiness, both for individuals and for those around them, was to be found in adapting or adjusting to their external circumstance, the reality around them. It was not their place or in their interest to question that reality. All attempts at seeking to redefine things could only end badly for those who tried. The model had little room for the possibility that this very same external world to which everyone was compelled to adapt and adjust could in itself be the problem – the source of all the suffering and affliction that posed myriad challenges to the individuals compelled to live, survive and reproduce that asphyxiating reality. Challenging though it was for the masses to be rational, the model on the other hand tended to be overly generous with how much rationality it credited the ruling and economic elite. Was this just salesmanship or did the psychoanalyst truly believe in a rational economic and political elite? Were they simply willing to project some of their rationality as psychoanalysts to the political and business leaders for whom they consulted as public relations professionals and image makers? Put differently, did the psychoanalysts really credit any other profession or group of social actors with rationality but themselves? Their power to define and confine rationality as they saw fit meant that, at the end of the day, the capacity to be rational was theirs to certify, dish out and withdraw as they saw fit. Because they had the support and protection of the powerful business and political elite, they could afford to be generous in turn to the politicians and businessmen and -women with whom they rubbed shoulders and strategised on how to keep the masses apparently happy and truly docile.[97]

When the heavily funded research failed to yield results of significant promise, faith in psychologists and their enthusiastic recipes started to dwindle. Even among psychologists themselves, there was growing recognition of just how difficult it was to understand and control the inner workings of the human mind. The fact that every mind, however unschooled and undomesticated, is not completely devoid of rationality, speaks to the dangers of artificially creating cleavages between the masses and the elite by defining and confining rational and irrationally in mindlessly dichotomous ways. Voices were rising to urge caution and mitigate extravagant claims. The mind, even when owned by the purported simple-minded working class masses of the industrialised societies or by the so-called primitive savages of the distant lands peopled by the non-Western 'other', was proving to be far more complex than it had been portrayed. Apparently, there were no simple solutions for the problems of the supposedly simple-minded, despite the control craved by psychoanalysts on behalf of their powerful political and economic clients. If there was rather little to their grand theories of the mind on how, in practical terms, to manage the dangerous irrational forces of human beings, what was the point of continuing to respect psychoanalysts and their offerings? Was there any reason to continue trusting them and their recommendation that democracy was best achieved not by listening to the people and following their choices but by letting an authoritarian elite tell them directly or subliminally what to think and how to think, what do and how to do it (Mills 1956)?[98]

Why should psychoanalysis operate on the preconception that suffering is a mistake, a kind of weakness or an illness? Pain is part and parcel of life, to be embodied and reproduced as memory and in the service of adaptability. Suffering lies at the heart of some of the greatest of life's truths. Instead of seeking to undo suffering or to erase it from human experience as the psychoanalysts tended to suggest, was it not more realistic to make it inform human lives? Is there really much justification in thinking in terms of controlling than freeing human beings into defining themselves?[99] Instead of defining and confining one another, would individuals and societies not fulfil themselves better if people were free to define and empower themselves, to the best of their abilities, through their joys and their pains? Is rationality really meaningful divorced from the emotional containers and contexts that make rationality possible? How realistic is it to conjure up an entirely out of body experience of a mind and thinking self of the type suggested by René Descartes's *Cogito Ergo Sum*?

The idea of human nature that is deep and layered has never been in doubt. What theorists, thinkers and people in general have tended to disagree on is the essential content of that human nature. What does one get if one patiently peels layer after layer of human nature, until the end, a kernel of sorts, where peeling is no longer possible? Is it a reservoir of benevolence, enlightenment, nourishment and happiness, or is it an abyss of darkness, danger, violence, evil and bitterness, or is it a nuanced and intricate blend of both? Is it imbued with a clear sense of right and wrong, good and bad or muddled up in indiscernible ways? The Freudians were clearly of the conviction that the hidden constitutive forces of human nature were more threatening and violent than peaceful and inviting. With the demise of the Freudians came the rise to power of those who believed that Freud and his followers were wrong about human nature.

Prominent among Freud's critics was Wilhelm Reich, who had originally been a devoted disciple of Freud in Vienna in the 1920s, until he challenged Freud over the fundamental basis of psychoanalysis. Reich believed the complete opposite of what Freud and his followers believed. Where Freud saw and faulted the maladjusted individual for their uncontrolled violent, warlike raging inferno of emotions, Reich saw the initial goodness of individuals corrupted by a highly repressive society and social order. To Reich, the unconscious forces inside the human mind were good. It was their repression by society that distorted the goodness and made people dangerous. The society (and by extension the economic and ruling elite), not the individual and the masses, were to blame for any signs of violence, maladjustment and threat to established order (the status quo) displayed by the individual and the masses. Reich and his followers believed that the way to build a better society was to let the self free but what they didn't realise is that this idea of liberation would provide business and politics with yet another way to control the self by feeding its infinite desires. Like Freud's other critics, Reich advocated the liberation of the inner self from its continued repression and control. Individuals were encouraged to settle for nothing less than they could be, and to seek to achieve the best possible for themselves. It was only by letting the inner self rise and flourish that human beings could become stronger and society better. Liberation took the form of bringing out suppressed feelings and memories through such acts as screaming, crying and anger, as well as the release of libidinal, sexual energy. Reich and his followers believed that neurosis were due to lack of orgasm. Sexual freedom was the recipe for health (Reich 1946).[100]

Other critics of the Freudian psychoanalysts included Vance Packard, whose book, *The Hidden Persuaders* accused psychoanalysts of using their powers of manipulation and persuasion to reduce American citizens to passive emotional puppets confined to keeping their consumer palates active and accelerated in the interest of mass production and the profit margins of corporate America. They did this through the use of techniques that included subliminal stimulation and seduction to manipulate people's unconscious desires to create longings for the relentless proliferation of new brands and trademarks.

They had turned the population into unwitting participants and victims of *planned obsolescence*. This is a policy and practice by corporations of designing and making products with artificially limited useful lives, so they can become obsolete, unfashionable or no longer functional in time to send the consumer back shopping for replacements (Packard 1981[1957]).[101]

Another high profile critic was Herbert Marcuse, an influential philosopher and social critic with a background in psychoanalysis. A prominent theme in his book, *One-Dimensional Man* (Marcuse 1964), is his critique of the almost obsessive drive among psychoanalysts spearheaded by the likes of Anna Freud and public relations practitioners such as Bernays that it was desirable and in the best interest of civilisation to manipulate and control human nature. Marcuse criticised the manner advertising was used to manipulate and brainwash consumers, persuading them in subtle and underhand ways to embrace products and do things that were not entirely the result of their own free will. He did not take kindly to the cynical paternalism that ordinary humans and the consuming masses were simply beneath the rigorous expectations of being rational in thought and action. The obsession with putting profit against human dignity while pretending to be at the service of consumers and their desires worried him. All it did was to create docile one-dimensional, conformist and repressive citizens at the beck and call of corporate and state violence, illegalities and impunities. Eternal vulnerability was the real price paid by those manipulated into compliance with such expectations of the industries of desire and desirability. The psychoanalysts had become the corrupt agents of those who ruled America. Marcuse contested the idea that the deeper emotional drives of humans were inherently violent, evil and antisocial. To seek to reduce people to a one-dimensional calculous of a rationality that was more imagined than real, was in effect to produce people without the creative

60

innovativeness and improvisation that made them truly balanced and whole. To him, it was society that made human beings dangerous by repressing, distorting and negatively representing human nature. He criticised psychoanalysts for pandering to big business and to the political elite by suggesting that the corrupting violence and repression by society was justified. The intervention by psychoanalysts to prop up such problematic assumptions about human nature only made worse prevalent mechanisms to extract conformity from people willy-nilly and to create a one-dimensional society of one-dimensional citizens (Marcuse 2002[1964)].[102]

Some American student activists drew inspiration from Herbert Marcuse's teachings and writings. The students opted to resist instead of merely yielding to the whims and caprices of the status quo that urged them to tame the animal within them in the interest of stable and predictable social reproduction. They summed up the predicament of ordinary Americans with the slogan: "There is a policeman in all our heads, he must be destroyed";[103] a destruction that could come about through the overthrow of the state and the corporations that had engineered its internalisation and reproduction. But the American state fought back violently in vehement defence of the status quo. The force of the state was much bigger and stronger and powerful than the activists had realised. Despite their efforts, the activists eventually reached the conclusion that it was impossible to get the policeman out of one's head by overthrowing the state. Each and every one had to get into their own minds instead and remove the controls implanted there by the state, the corporations and their enablers in public relations and the mass media. This, they hoped, would give rise to a new self, a new culture and a new society. Personal and social transformation could not be divorced from each other. The personal was inevitably political. Without changing the personal, there was little chance of changing the political. To seek autonomy was to take ownership of one's freedom and of one's person. It was paramount to explore ways of freeing oneself from the controls implanted in one's mind by society and its instances of social control, so one could be able to express one's true inner self without inhibitions.[104]

The fact that a current of Freudian psychoanalysts had actively colluded with the state and its instances of legitimation had only made people more dangerous. Martin Luther King Jr was equally critical, drawing extensively from the experience of African Americans perceived and related to as outsiders within American society and its dominant white value system. He took issue with the terms "maladjusted" and "maladjustment", terms often used to describe African Americans in a highly racialised and segregated American society, pregnant with social, economic and political inequalities. King argued that individuals so depicted were far from maladjusted. It was the corrupt, evil and corrupting segregated and hierarchised society they lived in that was maladjusted and that desperately needed transformation to become truly inclusive, participatory and just. Like Marcuse, King switched the source of evil from an inward conflict in struggling individuals to the maladjustment of the society itself. If the society was sick, to blame was the society itself and not its inhabitants. As King put it in a 1963 speech delivered at Western Michigan University, being maladjusted, as psychologists love to say, is not always a bad thing. In some instances, it is actually desirable to be maladjusted, especially as a form of resistance to discrimination and injustice, and in situations where being adjusted only serves the interest of the dominant, the powerful and the privileged. He challenged people of goodwill to openly display their maladjustment to the injustices and inequalities of the world until societies were truly transformed for the betterment of all and sundry.[105]

Such mounting accusations of seeking to promote repressive forms of social control may have seriously dented but did not completely erase the reputation and political influence of Freudian psychoanalysis.[106] It should come as no surprise to anyone in the academy, especially those of us in the Global South or as outsiders within the academy in Europe and North America that a theory and a practice criticised do not necessarily die. An estranged theory could be driven underground, resort to hibernation or, in a world of hierarchies, ambitions of dominance, mobility and unequal encounters, it could be exported. In a world where race, place, culture, gender, sex and age matter and richly determine perception and social visibility, the death or demise of a theory in one instance does not immediately translate, if ever it does, into its death in another category and set of relationships. Thus, for instance, the fact that in 21st century America, African Americans still feel aggrieved enough to rally around the slogan of "Black Lives Matter" means that the alleged demise of the Freudian theory of hidden dangerous forces in society needing to be controlled, could not have applied across the board, and if it did apply, it couldn't have been to the same degree across the racially segregated divide. It is not unheard of, in this day and age of the proliferation of video clips and excerpts of text, to come across an anonymous text such as: "Our greatest power over Blacks is that we control everything they believe. We control their education, their news media, their entertainment, all their statistics, and even their images of themselves. This therefore allows us to inundate Blacks with disinformation designed to instil the myth of white superiority and Black hatred into their minds. It's a psychological warfare program used for protecting our white dominance."[107] Resilient images of Africa as a dark continent peopled by primitive savages living in jungles or, to quote Donald Trump, "Shithole countries",[108] are an added illustration that theories of domination die hard, and that their presumed death in one context should not necessarily be extrapolated to mean their death everywhere.

5

Freedom at Last or Wolves of Repression in Sheepskin?

Some people are reluctant to condone the degree of cynicism towards rationality and popular participatory democracy displayed by Bernays and the Freudian psychoanalysts. They not only refuse to see rationality and democracy as being in short supply – something to be claimed mostly in abstraction because of the hidden dangerous forces in human beings (the masses in particular) that threaten the materialisation of rationality and democracy in real terms – they believe the contrary: that human beings are, in reality, essentially rational beings. If human rationality is threatened by dangerous forces lurking just beneath the surface of the accepted order, could not science be deployed to penetrate the unconscious and explore ways of salvaging rationality from the forces that are determined to undermine and neutralise it? And if it is possible to know exactly what and how people feel and why they feel the way they do, as Bernays confidently claimed and built his public relations empire around the idea, could ways not be devised to seek to reassure them so they never give up on rationality, the very foundation of the civilisation that tagged them along and with which they were expected to identify? And in this way, would it not be possible to prevent their anger and frustrations with their political, economic and cultural leadership and governing institutions from boiling over? If all of these were possible, would it make sense to continue to argue and insist that democracy and freedom of choice are impracticable in a mass society?[109]

With every challenge in a creative society, a hero springs to the fore with Superman or Spiderman reassurance. In this instance, George Horace Gallup, an American journalism professor and practitioner with a background in psychology keen on understanding public opinion as a measure of the pulse of democracy with scientific precision using statistical and survey methods, stood up to be counted upon as the hero of the moment (Gallup and Rae 1968). He came up with an answer that parted ways with Bernays's cynicism and opportunism. Instead of portraying people as being at the mercy of unconscious forces and therefore in need to be controlled, Gallup devised a system of opinion polling and mass observational surveys of the type pioneered in Britain by the likes of Tom Harrison (Harrison 1987, 2011[1976]; Hubble 2006), underpinned by the assumption that people could be trusted to know their everyday experiences and what they wanted, instead of being manipulated with options that they did not really want or desire, if left to figure things out for themselves (Gallup and Rae 1968).[110] He operated on the basis that if people absolutely did not want to buy a product or subscribe to a political option and candidate, no amount of advertising, marketing or public relations would make them do it. Gallup and his collaborators argued that one could measure and predict the opinions and behaviour of the public if one asked strictly factual questions and avoided manipulating their emotions. Facts mattered, and facts were all that was needed to choose the right and logical line of action. As many a journalist who believes in objectivity, Gallup was of the conviction that facts could speak for themselves. Facts did not need embellishments. Emotions and Facts could not be good bedfellows. The challenge was thus to devise ways of asking questions that elicited the facts of any given situation, irrespective of what different parties thought, felt or desired about the facts (Gallup and Rae 1968; Ohmer 2006).[111]

The rise of scientific polling spearheaded by Gallup was intended to debunk the prevalent views, especially in elite political circles, that the public could not be trusted. Thanks to

Bernays and his public relations enterprises, prior to the advent of scientific polling, it was commonplace in decision making circles to dismiss public opinion as irrational, ill-informed, chaotic and unruly. Scientific polling took the opposite view. It basically assumed people to be essentially rational beings who were more inclined to making good decisions. With this confidence in rational beings making rational choices, came a renewed confidence in democracy as a system of government informed by public opinion, freedom of expression and participation for all and sundry. If people were basically to be trusted as rational beings, if they were no longer irrational consumers consumed by dangerous desires, then there was little justification to distance politicians from the masses, since the latter were in every way sensible citizens qualified to partake in the managing of their public affairs. Since their inception, Gallup polls have played a significant role in successive American elections, in general, and in presidential elections, in particular (Newport et al. 2009).[112]

If the Freudians had tried and failed to make the individual do the bidding of society and its economic and socio-political elites, what could be better than simply letting the defiant individual have his or her way? Put differently, if the dictatorship or prescriptiveness of the elite had proved itself to be too overwhelming, why not swing to the other end of the pendulum by exploring the potentials of the all-powerful individual? In the spirit of zero-sum games, why not yield completely to the absolute autonomy of the individual and its fundamentalist crusaders? Bouncing from one end of the pendulum to the other was the name of the game of dichotomies. There was scant patience for compromise in this bazaar of absolutes. The new and winning psychological recipe of the day − the rhetoric of unmitigated freedom − was to be served to all who came to seek assistance with placing products and selling their political platforms and messages to voters, would be techniques for recognising and providing for a new autonomous being free of all social constraints, an all-powerful being strong enough to humble tradition and the status quo. What could be better than swinging from elitism gone rogue to individualism gone rogue? Whatever became of the truism that the pendulum swings to the right and to the left and seems to find its way back to something like dead centre?[113]

The new individual expected to be targeted as an autonomous or independent individual, and not as part of an assumed or concocted collectivity, community or society. If products have always been emotional, the new individual wanted his or her products specifically tailored or targeted to suit his/her every whim and caprice as individual. Corporations and politicians were compelled to conform to this new nonconformist individual. The new consumer king whose every desire was law, could be likened to junky or monster of freedoms, rights and entitlement without responsibilities, ready to demolish all hurdles on the way to the gratification of the self. This was the crystallisation of the individual as the beginning and end of all. It highlighted the myths of the fixed self and of society as little more than the sum total of the individuals who constituted it. There was no such thing as society. Individuals were the only unit of analysis that mattered, and it needed to be reiterated ad nauseam that thinking of and being preoccupied with oneself, far from being an act of selfishness or a case of extreme self-love, was actually the highest duty any individual could perform. If politics was relevant, the individual was the start point and the end point of politics. Individuals did not need society to be who they were, what they were and how they were.[114]

Values and lifestyle marketing was designed to target this new individual who was best categorised by different psychological desires and drives rather than by social class, gender and age. Emphasis was on the psychological determinants of the hierarchy of needs that had a bearing on individual self-actualisation, self-direction free of societal interference and prescriptiveness. As individuals, they were defined by the choices they made and not by the diktats of society. To the inner directors among them, personal satisfaction was more valued than class and status. Personal experience mattered a great deal. A technique employed in value and lifestyle studies is to ask people the same question over and over and over again, getting deeper and deeper with every answer received, purportedly questing for the assumed kernel at the core of the person. Some of those involved in such surveys have employed, rightly or wrongly, the metaphor of peeling an onion to imply a determined effort to reach the "real core" of the person under documentation by taking off protective layer after protective layer, of thoughts, feelings, believes and practices until one is satisfied that one has harvested a thick description of self-articulations to build a profile on.[115]

The invention of values and lifestyles studies exploded in a vast industry of psychological market research in which the technique of the focus group invented by Freudian psychoanalysts in the 1950s to allow patients (and subsequently consumers) to express their inner feelings and needs was integrated and reinvented. While the focus group was initially aimed at persuading real or potential consumers to purchase a limited range of mass-produced goods, the use of the focus group in value and lifestyles studies was motivated by the need to explore the inner feelings of lifestyle groups as the basis for the invention of new ranges of products that would allow those groups to express what they felt was their individuality. This innovative approach was able to attract consumers who had previously rebelled against the conformity imposed by consumerism (designed to give individuals the illusion of control, while enabling and promoting real control and the management of society by an economic elite), because they now saw it as being about themselves as autonomous beings seeking self-realisation on their own terms. People who had wanted to have both life and politics on their own terms were attracted. They saw themselves as autonomous powerful individuals entitled to be respected and entitled to have the best in terms of consumer products, public and private services such as health and education. It was the method, par excellence, of voicing the voiceless, not as social categories, but as questing and thirsting individuals whose aspirations and desires knew no bounds.[116]

True to its image as an eternal winner, capable of profiting from its supporters and its critiques alike, capitalism found a way of cashing in on the all-powerful individual just as it had cashed in on the all-powerful elite society. The perceived successes of the values and lifestyles technique were embraced by capitalism to proliferate the development of products that evoked a much more elastic or infinite sense of self that aspired and was encouraged to aspire to be anything it wanted to be. The products were purposefully intended to foster that limitless self. They were not just products that were sold to the individual. Also sold to the individual was a way of life, a way of being and a system of values. And, with this, came the notion that identities could be literally bought or acquired through what one consumed, how one consumed and the cultivated and internalised sense of who one was from one's consumer practices and attitudes. Identities were not something one was born with or something tied to the class, gender or social categories into which one was fitted by criteria established and implemented by forces or instances outside of one's control, but rather they were something one was perfectly free to create and recreate, ad infinitum. The world was there in the palm of the individual to configure and reconfigure as he/she saw fit, and in tune with his/her every whim and caprice. Never, never again, would the individual be made to think little or less of him/herself. He/she must rise and embrace his/her self-belief. It was the advent of the all-powerful individual – the individual as consumer king at the centre and calculus of society, and of every political, economic and social action.[117]

The advent of information and communication technologies such as the computer, the internet, global consumer television and social media (e.g. Facebook, Twitter and Instagram) have only expanded further the horizons of this new individualism, even if not always at the service of democracy (McChesney 2013, 2015). Short runs of consumer products are now easily produced thanks to the computer, and this has reduced the amount of goods that are mass produced and stockpiled in warehouses. With the new self and with computer facilitation, not only is production more tailored to suit the tastes of particular individual consumers, production can go on nonstop in response to a consumer desire without limits. There is as much demand as there are individuals with particular, peculiar and ever-changing needs and tastes, desires and consumer aspirations. The explosion of desire has brought about a never-ending consumer boom. Corporations have realised that it is in their interest to encourage people to feel and explore their uniqueness of being. Instead of seeking to discourage consumers with a contrived conformism, corporations have now settled for accompanying and assisting consumers in their endless personal journeys of self-exploration and self-actualisation. The business elite at the head of corporations have realised that far from being a threat, rebelling against conformity the way some individuals have done, has instead turned out to be their greatest opportunity. This has been depicted as the triumph of the self and of self-indulgence, and as rightly so, especially by those who believe that there is no such thing as society, over and above the sum total of individuals pursuing very personal interests, making personal choices and seeking their very own wellbeing.[118]

Again, just like capitalism, psychologists were there to cash in, not only economically, but in terms of the power this new technology brought them to influence politics and decision making in the wider American society and globally. The psychologists behind the techniques for measuring the values and lifestyle priorities of the new self-absorbed individual soon manoeuvred themselves into very powerful positions where they could predict what new product self-actualisers would choose. Soon, they were able to demonstrate that they could predict not just the products that the self-actualisers would buy, but also the politicians for whom they would vote. Politicians who had depended on their bases and on constituencies configured into social categories informed by such indicators as race, geography/constituency, class, gender and age, would soon realise that they could not win elections on the basis of such traditional conventional indicators cultivated over the years. Winning and losing would depend more than ever before on the extent to which a politician was able or not to harness the swing voters, not as social categories, but as individuals with unique desires and expectations, hopes and fears. For these psychologists in the business of moulding and selling politicians to the electorate, to profile a candidate meant to package and present that candidate as the best solution to fulfilling the whims and caprices of each and every member of the electorate, whims and caprices which were often hidden beneath the superficialities of rationalist political discourses and rhetoric. If the individual had become the consumer king with corporations and big business working round the clock to satisfy their every desire, what politics needed as well were politicians bending over backwards to satisfy every political whim and caprice of the consumer citizen (as king) on whose vote politicians depended to access the political power they sought. The only idea of society (if the term must be used) that the autonomous consumer citizen was prepared to settle for was a society in which their needs and desires as individuals were read and fulfilled without prejudice in the manner that business had proved it could in a free market context. Somehow, these psychologists had engineered an unproblematised understanding of the free market as free of ideology and political interference, and as driven entirely by the diktats of sovereign individual consumers (Marcuse 2002[1964]; Goodwin et al. 1997; Chomsky 1999, 2002; Tye 1998; Featherstone 2007; Nichols and McChesney 2013; McChesney 2015).[119]

Ronald Reagan, President of the USA from 1980 to 1988, was the first politician to seek to make political capital of the new self and inner-directed individual. Taking advantage of television as the most adept medium of communication in his day, as well as of his reputation as "The Great Communicator" (Denton 1988), Reagan promised to take the lead in taking government off the back of Americans and freeing up individuals to rise and shine as only they knew best. His campaign was predicated upon the idea that too much government was dangerous for the people, who should be allowed to make the basic decisions. Bureaucrats and centralised government had to get out of the way, so people could experience the thrills and successes of running things themselves, taking control of their own destiny and moving power out of the hands of the *deep state* (Klaas 2017; Corsi 2018; Jarrett 2018; Pirro 2018) that tended to be remote and insensitive to the everyday challenges confronting the very people they purportedly cared for and cared about. His was a clarion call for the death of society and its technologies of repression. Reagan basically spearheaded an age-old American argument that hard work paid off, and no one should feel guilty for working hard, especially not towards their lazy compatriots who aspired to and desired little beyond handouts. He urged hardworking Americans not to throw away their hard-earned money and not to feel guilty for refusing to throw it away on those who chose to remain unemployed, homeless and dependent on state-run social welfare programmes. He made the denial of compassion respectable, and encouraged the rich who, through their hard work had earned the right to have better jobs, send their children to better schools, contribute less for healthcare and benefit more from tax cuts not to feel guilty about their entitlements.[120]

In his valorisation and celebration of individualism and individual self-actualisation, Reagan found a partner and staunch supporter who was determined to follow him to the end of the world under the new form of democracy that he had personally engineered.[121] Her name was Margaret Thatcher, who served as Prime Minister of the UK from 1979 to 1990 and as leader of the Conservative Party from 1975 to 1990 (Wapshott 2007). Like Reagan's, Thatcher's vision of society was one in which the wants and desires of all and sundry, taken individually, are satisfied by a free, truly deregulated market. She had little patience for what others called society; all she saw were individuals going about the business of self-actualisation. Like Reagan as well, she was decidedly convinced that government was not the solution to the challenges facing the people but the problem. The slimmer the government and the weaker its capacities to interfere with the economy beyond providing an ordered deregulated environment for free market enterprise, the better for the wellbeing of individuals and their country. She recruited American style advertisers such as Saatchi & Saatchi as consultants to run, in collaboration with her newly created Centre for Policy Studies, focus groups for her party with the British electorate.[122] They were tasked with finding out what the people as individuals really wanted, and to work with her and the conservative party to make those wants materialise in the lives of the people. Just as in America, the aim of the focus groups was not to make people talk rationally about their thoughts, feelings and desires, but rather, to reveal their inner desires and emotions about politicians and government, freedom and money.[123]

The underlying aim was to encourage people to express themselves and to resist central government control more, because the individual was and should rightly be the centre of focus. Government was to be treated as a disease for which it pretends to be a cure. The state should be nothing but a humble servant of the people, and not the overbearing master that it tended to be. Put differently, the state was game to be stalked, captured and harnessed for their self-actualisation by ambitious individuals as they absolutely saw fit. People had to be liberated to express themselves as individuals, to have their own personalities, to be their own men and women, and not to be constantly presented and exploited as statistics and as part of an amorphous collectivity, crowd or some such nebulous category as class, age and sex. The private sector of corporations and businesses, big and small, operating in a free and truly deregulated arena, was best suited to give the people – unapologetically independent, self-absorbed, self-indulging and all-consuming individuals – their every affordable consumer desire and aspiration. The idea was to replace the nebulous notion of society with the actual unit of analysis for everything – the individual in his/her infinite multiplicities, and as an embodiment of needs, wants and desires, hopes and fears.[124] As Margaret Thatcher captured it, not only are individuals unequal, everyone has a right to be unequal, and every human being is equally valued in the eyes of truly democratic consumer capitalism.[125]

Initially, in both the USA and the UK, Reagan and Thatcher's opponents, mostly left leaning political parties and politicians, criticised their new individualism and idea of democracy as the very epitome of a cynical devotion to the most selfish and greedy aspects of human nature. To their critics, both Reagan and Thatcher had killed society with excessive individualism, by insisting on a notion of society that was seldom larger than the individual. How could society be possible if people were seen and treated as little more than self-seeking emotional isolated individuals? How could society be possible without a commitment to a robust public sphere, however contested, where ideas could be seriously debated to inform a carefully distilled and negotiated consensus on a shared vision and sense of a common purpose, public options and policies (Habermas 1989; Goode 2005; Johnson 2006)? As Tony Blair, a former Prime Minister of Britain and leader of the Labour Party has been questioning with the growth of right wing and left wing populism and exclusionary fundamentalism in identity politics in Britain, the USA and elsewhere: how exactly is a shared social truth possible without a semblance of social consensus?[126] The left-leaning politicians like Tony Blair were perplexed that Reagan and Thatcher were actually winning elections repeatedly through dissuading people from thinking that there were such things as common interests, and as having to warm up to the idea of collective success through helping one another to rise above individual feelings and fear of belonging and aspiring together. It is noteworthy that this is also the period of rising rational choice and methodological individualism (empiricism) in the social sciences. Although facts are said to matter and to speak for themselves, there is increasingly little consideration for the fact that not all that counts can be counted and not all that can be counted counts.[127]

However, as they repeatedly lost elections under the rising popularity of the new individualism, the Democratic Party and the Labour Party in the USA and the UK, respectively, found themselves compelled to sacrifice some of their more progressive pro-society, pro-socialist, pro-welfare policies and ideologies in order to appeal to the swing voters who value and lifestyle focus groups surveys had repeatedly demonstrated no longer voted according to such indicators as social solidarity, social class and social status. The swing voter had come to think and behave like a consumer, who was only interested in having his or her consumer instincts satisfied, and not in such things as ideology, even as they were being manipulated for clearly ideological ends. They were also encouraged to cultivate indifference to *Ubuntu*, with its roots in human sociality, solidarity and inclusivity (Nyamnjoh 2015). If anything, the swing voter was challenging every politician to turn politics into a form of consumer business or forever perish. Democracy had to follow consumer rules in a context of consumer capitalism. Democrats in the US such as Bill Clinton (President from 1992 to 2000) and UK Labour politicians such as Tony Blair (Prime Minister from 1997 to 2007 and leader of the Labour Party from 1994 to 2007) decided to meet halfway the Reagan and Thatcher doctrine of the centrality of the individual and their satisfaction, happiness and wellbeing. This decision came even at the cost of much uproar among and accusations of betrayal by their more traditional and more ideologically commitment fellow party members. The thinking of candidates seeking to be elected in both parties was simple. Having noticed that they had lost ground even among traditional Labour and Democrat voters to the Conservative and Republican parties, the Democrat and Labour leadership (Clinton and Blair respectively) knew it was adapt or perish. They either perished or took seriously the idea of individuals who no longer saw themselves in terms of group membership but purely in terms of political consumers who were entitled to demand things in return from politicians for the taxes and obligations they had paid and fulfilled by voting them into office. Their choice to adapt could be seen as the crowning glory of the triumph of the new individualism as well as of the dominant order in business and in government to think of and relate to individuals as purely emotional beings who had needs and wants and desires that needed satisfaction and could be satisfied unconsciously. Reagan's and Thatcher's opponents had finally caught up with their idea that the individual is more important than society, even if it means the death of the latter.[128]

Henceforth, politicians in the USA and the UK would all be united around the core principles that the individual, not so much society, is the central focus. The central premise is that politics is not so much about making rational decisions, but rather about harkening to the whims and caprices of the electorate, not as a collectivity, but as a sea of individuals with the unique and personalised sea of hopes and fears and desires. Instead of being puppets subject to manipulation of politicians, the individual had become like a puppet owner with competing politicians at their disposal, keeping each and every one of them on their toes, dancing around nonstop to satisfy his/her every desire[129]. The listening, nimble-footed, accommodating and ideological supple politician is the one who succeeds with the individual and dispersed electorate unified in nothing else but the trinity of the *selfie*: "Me, Myself and I" (Storr 2018; Kuntsman 2017).

In this regard, it could be argued that democracy becomes exaggeratedly little more than suspending rationality and relentlessly pandering to the hidden, complex, layered and ever-multiplying desires of the elusive individual who seeks freedoms without many responsibilities in return. The politician, who has reduced democracy to elections, being elected and re-elected, does not need to be personally aware of all these hopes, fears, desires harboured by the all-powerful individual consumer and voter. All such a politician has to do is to outsource the production and weaponisation of such knowledge to the marketing and public relations consultants, whose business it is to get into the heads of individuals, discover what they want politicians to do that appeals to them as individuals, tap into and harness such desires as targeted election themes for the satisfaction of their political clients and for their own personal enrichment as psychologists at the service of politics. Themes that do not appeal to the swing voters are sacrificed, regardless or not whether such themes constitute core principles for the candidate and/or party seeking electability. With the data collected, the values and lifestyle pollster could easily kill two birds with one stone by using the same information to entice corporations to create and manufacture new ranges of products that allow swing voters to express their individuality even more.[130] Is this what the likes of Cambridge Analytica and Facebook are all about when they cosy up and cuddle one another like porcupines in winter, harvesting and sharing the personal data of millions of users the world over attracted by their promise of freedom and democracy?

If the criticism brought to bear on him as presidential candidate and subsequently as President of the USA following the 2016 elections is anything to go by, it could be argued that Donald Trump epitomises the new individualism taken to the limit. Not only did Trump vigorously support Reagan's "Make America Great Again" campaign for president in the 1980s, he was inspired by Reagan along with Norman Vincent Peale's book, *The Power of Positive Thinking* (his childhood family bible), to dream and work towards becoming America's president one day. It is thus hardly surprising that some have referred to Donald Trump as the second coming of Ronald Reagan. Like Reagan, Trump changed his party affiliation from Democrat to Republican. As a consummate performance artist, a master communicator, and a very talented messenger in his own right,[131] Trump has, however, done more than give Reagan and his new individualism a rebirth. With his penchant for anti-establishmentalism, distaste for elite politics and scant regard for political correctness, Trump has taken Ronald Reagan's and Margaret Thatcher's cynicism about normalised society to higher heights – striving for "glorious" isolation, nativism, narrow nationalism, populism and ever-diminishing circles of inclusion, while actively subverting globalism (McCain 2018) – and all the way from a purportedly "consummate self-made" man and billionaire to a supposedly "self-made" President who reportedly seems to care little about whom he offends (with the exception of Vladimir Putin of Russia), kills everything he touches and burns everyone who comes anywhere near him (Wilson 2018).[132] Not only is there no such thing as society

79

with him, there is no opinion, vision, mission, higher loyalty, or anyone else who counts and matters but Donald J. Trump and the self-aggrandising opportunities he craves. Like Louis XIV of France who claimed to be the state (*l'état, c'est moi*) (Claydon and Levillain 2015), Trump is America and America is Trump. And like Jesus Christ, Trump may well be, in the estimation of his fervent Evangelical Christians support base in particular, "the way, the truth and the light".[133] His slogan of "Make America Great Again", can be understood ultimately, as a call to "Make Trump Great Again". He is the product of the combined efforts of American capitalism, American consumerism and American democracy on the one hand, and their hidden persuaders in the world of advertisement and public relations on the other (Dionne Jr. et al. 2017).[134] In the spirit of the new individualism, he loves striking deals and making money for himself and his immediate family, and would do anything not to lose his place in the world rankings of top billionaires (Trump with Schwartz 1987; Ross with McLean 2005; Trump with McIver and Kiyosaki with Lechter 2006; Trump with McIver 2007, 2008; Johnston 2016; Fox 2018).

Trump's critics say he is without substance if one scratches below the surface, that he has no core beliefs and that he grabs everything and anything and agrees with everyone. He agrees with whoever is the last person to speak to him. He has no policy positions. He postures rather than acts in accordance with principles. He has no sense of reality or limitations, and struggles to distinguish fact from fiction. All he cares about is being loved and being liked,[135] despite being hateful, vile and racist or racially ignorant. He is untrustworthy, not dependable, unfit to be President, and daily demeans the presidency and undermines the rule of law by his determined and persistent attacks on the *deep state* (Department of Justice, FBI and related intelligence and national security services).[136] He is said to be cantankerous and easy to anger, and to thump his chest and bluster as if he was anything but a physical and emotional coward. Above all, he is said to live either in fear of Putin and Russia or in service to both.[137] He cannot stand the prolonged contestation of his electoral victory or the fact that Russian meddling with the election in his favour may have played a crucial role in his victory. Despite the conclusion to the contrary by all state intelligence agencies, he continues to claim emphatically that there was no Russian meddling and that his campaign did not collude with Russia to influence the outcome of the election (Johnston 2016; Brazile 2017; Clinton 2017; Harding 2017; Clapper with Brown 2018; Comey 2018; Frum 2018; Hayden 2018; Isikoff and Corn 2018; Klaas 2017; Mcfaul 2018; Nance 2018; Snyder 2018; Watts 2018; Wolff 2018).[138] Trump has stood his ground (Jarrett 2018; Pirro 2018) despite reportedly being shown, two weeks before his inauguration, "highly classified intelligence indicating that President Vladimir V. Putin of Russia had personally ordered complex cyberattacks to sway the 2016 American election".[139] This stubborn insistence by Trump and stiff resistance to openly and unequivocally criticise Vladimir Putin, has drawn rare public condemnation from some of his fellow Republicans. One of them, Will Hurd, has concluded that "Trump Is Being Manipulated by Putin", arguing that "By playing into Vladimir Putin's hands", Trump, as "the leader of the free world" is actively participating in a Russian disinformation campaign and legitimising Russian denial and weakening the credibility of the United States to both its friends and foes abroad. Hurd called on fellow members of congress to join him in fulfilling their "oversight duty as well as keep the American people informed of the current danger".[140]

If Michael Wolff, author of *Fire and Fury: Inside the Trump Without House* (2018) is right, it would appear that Trump is clearly not fit to be the President of the USA. His ability to ingest and digest information is clearly not there. He doesn't read or even skim. He is no more than semi-literate. Indeed,

Wolff is damning in his portrayal of Trump, and so are many of the other commentators I have followed on TV. He is said to be like a tantrum-throwing toddler or a child needing instant gratification. Some have likened him to an adult trapped in the mind and attitudes of a juvenile or moron, who is interested neither in self-cultivation nor in the cultivation of others. It has also been said, not in whispers and not only by Wolff, that Trump suffers from attention-span deficits, and that he is incredibly thin skinned, of questionable competency as President, and obsessive and disrespectful of the very institutions he is expected to protect. Trump offers a perfect example of what one gets with the new individualism pushed to the extreme. When the individual is completely driven by his/her unconscious desires, fears and anger, has no loyalties whatsoever, but to him/herself, and whose only responsibility, if any, is to him/herself. Unlike Bernays who believed in a rational elite, Trump does not believe in anything but himself – his manipulative self. His attacks on the *deep state* (Corsi 2018; Klaas 2017; Jarrett 2018; Pirro 2018) on his Republican Party elite, on the Democrats, the media and almost everyone who does not do his bidding, with the exception of his most immediate family perhaps, including even Steve Bannon, "his evil genius" – as opposed to himself as the "stable genius" – (Green 2017; Koffler 2017) is ample evidence of the extreme insensitivities of the unconscious unchained and reigning supreme. This should however not be taken to imply that Bernays was any less full of himself. He thought of himself in a manner that would strike one as Trumpian. At the office, he saw himself as "the idea man, the star" (Tye 1998: 142), "demanded excellence and obeisance", claimed credit without giving any and could be "unforgiving" to staff who failed to live up to his expectations (Tye 1998: 44). His staff members were:

... limited to supporting roles, listening but seldom responding, all chairs, eyes, and ears zeroed in on Eddie. After all, he was the one who'd landed the clients, and he was responsible for keeping them satisfied. He'd concocted the strategies and mapped out tactics. He alone knew what it took to get things done and to pay the bills. As in many offices that revolve around a charismatic personality, he gave the orders and surrounded himself with people who were willing to carry them out. And like others who had launched their own empires, he ruled with an imperial air that sometimes crossed over into meanness (Tye 1998: 142).

If these damning assessments with Freudian libidinal undertones are true, even as the President might think or feel differently, then, how can an almighty giant of a country like the USA hope to be able to navigate the nuanced complexities of life, power and ambition in the 21st century with a reckless, self-absorbed simpleton at its helm? How can the leader of the most powerful country in the world be so ill-equipped to understand and act accordingly and strategically in tune with the truism that information and informed decisions and options are categorical imperatives? Isn't his failure to rise to the task and assume the challenges of his office a recipe for the end of American might as the rest of the world has been compelled to understand it? Does it really serve America's best civilisational interests, the imperative for social cohesion and global ambitions of dominance to reach out and surrender centuries of hard-earned rights and freedoms, power, privilege and pursuit of the good life for all and sundry without prejudice to Reagan's new individualism gone rogue? Is the ultimate prize of new individualism unavoidably such lacks in basic humanity, credibility and professionalism in leadership? Or could it be, as some Trump supporters would argue, that Trump, the penultimate new individualism President, is far more cunning, subtle, insightful and ruthless than some of his critics give him credit for?[141] Could all his apparent vices, contradictions, bungling, buffoonish sloppiness, utter disregard for the rule of law and display of admiration for dictators, personality cults and centralised state-own and government-controlled media in which everybody does the leader's bidding (Klaas 2017)[142] be nothing short of a carefully orchestrated propaganda and public relations strategy by Trump (in a manner that even an Edward Bernays would marvel at), to undermine all those – fellow Americans, American and global institutions, allies, media and critics – who dare to question his legitimacy and Humpty-Dumpty desire for total and unconditional loyalty from all and sundry (McCain 2018)?[143] If indeed so, this begs yet another perplexing question: How could Americans, aided by foreign interference or not, have settled for leadership and guidance from a performance artist who believes in little more than himself, who is without morality, ethics or scruple, who pays scant regard for the truth, and has no "higher loyalty" than himself (Comey 2018)? How could a man who promotes and protects himself first and foremost have risen through the ranks of the hierarchies of credibility and instances of legitimation of such a colossus of global power and influence that America attests to be, ambushing and wrecking with the reckless abandon of a tsunami, its core institutions and values: truth, democracy and a market economy? Could the engineering and perpetration of the consumer society and the consumer individual have ended up as little more than a freak and self-destructive experiment by a Frankenstein Monster of its very creation (Johnston 2016; Clapper with Brown 2018; Comey 2018; Frum 2018; Hayden 2018; Isikoff and Corn 2018; Marcotte 2018; Wolff 2018)?

In light of these developments, regardless of whether we are for or against Trump, it is worth asking the extent to which the values and lifestyle studies on the self-actualising individual yielded a more rounded consumer and political citizen? Has the application of psychological techniques in lifestyle studies with a focus on the inner driven autonomous individual done more than produce and sustain an isolated vulnerable and greedy self, claiming autonomy without responsibility? And what is there to substantiate the claim that this inner driven actualised self is any less open to manipulation by both business and politics? What arguments would those who believe in the reality of this self-actualised autonomous and expressive individual provide to counter the claim that the political and economic elite have just been as able to control him or her not by repressing them but by feeding their infinite greedy desires (Chomsky 2002; Tye 1998; Brock 2005; Nichols and McChesney 2013; McChesney 2015; Sherman 2017; Marcotte 2018)?

There is much food for thought, in the admission by Mark Zuckerberg, founder and CEO of Facebook, following the controversial 2016 presidential elections in the USA, elections which were interfered with by Russia and Cambridge Analytica in favour of Donald Trump. Initially, Zuckerberg had thought little of Facebook beyond seeing it as a social-networking tool to be made available as widely as possible for people to use as they saw fit. Following the controversy however, he admits: "... you can't just give people a voice ... You need to also make sure that the voice is not used for foreign interference in elections or disseminating fake news".[144] He realises, at long last, that freedom goes with responsibility, and that individual actors act within particular social contexts, with clear fields of actions and rules of the game. Society is after all not dead, even if it clearly is not all-powerful. There is need and an obligation for mutual accommodation and interdependence between the free, rights-craving and entitlement-driven individual, and society as facilitator, promoter and protector of the ideals of the imperative of having inclusive success and playing fields that are truly level.

Supposedly, by understanding and fulfilling the desires of individuals through the focus groups, the values and lifestyle psychology consultants were influencing politicians to give power to individuals and not to treat them as faceless groups who were told by politicians what was good for them. Who really – between the politician, the individual voter and the pollster psychologist – was *all-powerful* in this case remains an open question. Although, it could be argued, that none of them was really in charge, and that each simply gave the impression of being in charge by seeking to capitalise on what was really in charge: the individual's desires, hopes and fears. Each of them, the politician, the individual and the pollster psychologist was actively refusing to acknowledge their powerlessness in real terms by pretending that they, and they alone, had the final answer to the conundrum or predicament of being human through relationships with others in a world of a bewildering maze of contradictory whims and caprices, where power is at best a fleeting sensation of ownership and control.

6

Conclusion:
Beyond Impoverishing Dichotomies

To recapitulate, this essay has drawn on and fed into Adam Curtis's 2002 documentary – *The Century of the Self* – to argue that human nature has been characterised in Freudian theory and practices inspired therefrom by dichotomous thinking. One of such dichotomies is the contrast between humans as intrinsically rational (pursuit of self-interest) and humans as emotive creatures (jeopardising self-interest). More notably, rationality has been understood as imposing the higher order reasoning self on the more desire-based and emotive self. This is akin to a disciplining process. This dichotomy is productive of a normative argument and attendant hierarchies. To be civilised is to be rational (i.e. to discipline our desires) and for the most part we think that this is the cornerstone of civilisation. However, the essay also argues that claims of rationality are not often consistent with action. To allow for a modernity informed by bringing irrationality and rationality into conversation is to disabuse ourselves of a tendency towards a cynical, exclusionary and opportunistic perception of rationality. Thus, rather than setting up this impossible standard, or giving up on it entirely, we should see human beings as fluid in how they respond to situations (rationally or presumably irrationally), whether or not one agrees that emotions are necessarily irrational and rationality necessarily devoid of emotion.

The essay has taken issue with the often unproblematised normative implications of the distinction between rationality and irrationality. It questions the value system attached to the distinction (desirable/undesirable) and not necessarily the distinction itself, for we could just as easily switch the content of the labels. In the prism of such a value-laden distinction, socio-economic and political stability/order appears to be a function not of rationality but irrationality. In the political sense, we believe rationality is in short supply and must be manufactured or engineered by an elite credited with being rational. The essay has illustrated these points with examples from the political and economic realms. In both political and economic contexts, the essay appeals to the Freudian belief that we can never fully be civilised because a pernicious range of desires lurks deep within us, and every civilisation carries along its debris and malcontents. Economically, capitalism has exploited this basic irrationality of human beings. The result is an economic system that reveals only a pretentious interest in consumers as rational agents making rational decisions in a rational market and in a democratic society as the rational political arena, par excellence. What the system really wants is irrational people, and it exploits these irrationalities with its predilection for absolutes. Politically, there has been cynicism towards the idea that the masses have an inherent rationality. Rather, rationality is represented as a privileged position only attained by a well-schooled and thoroughly socialised political elite and their hidden persuaders – psychoanalysts, public relations professionals and advertisers (Packard 1981[1957]) who are superbly qualified to actively engineer or manufacture consent with or without subliminal and seductive messaging (Bernays 1947; The F. W. Faxon Company 1951; Herman and Chomsky 1988).[145] At best, we can hope to direct people towards enlightenment by playing on their irrationalities in order to steer them in the right direction. This represents a sort of disingenuous democracy, as democracy is both notionally and practically premised on the public use of reason. Even when opinion polls are apparently conducted on the basis of an assumption that people are rational and can be truthful and trusted to see clearly and pursue their best interests, the eventual outcome is the crystallisation and consolidation of an ethical heritage of individualism, where the individual reigns supreme – prescribing and/or confirming the death of society by projecting him/herself as the ultimate authority on what constitutes his/her self-interest; the thinking being that while the individual may take advice from others, no one knows more than the individual when it comes to that self-interest.

Drawing on the idea of the crossroads as mediator of encounters and facilitator of interconnections and interdependencies, as well as on the infinite capacity of crossroads to entertain and accommodate contradictions and incommensurability (Nyamnjoh 2017a, 2017[2015]b), the essay has argued that the answer to the tension between rationality and irrationality, nature and culture, individual and society lies neither with extreme repression nor with an abstract and exaggerated sense of freedom. It stresses that rationality and irrationality, reason and emotion, the mind and the heart are far more entangled than our propensity for dichotomisation accounts for. It is thus worth reiterating that emotions and rationality are both inherent attributes of human beings. The drive to control (nature, other humans, oneself) also has very universal human roots, probably stemming from the self-preservation instinct on which the disciplines of psychology and biology are quite instructive. Just like it is impossible to hide Stevenson's dangerous and violent Mr Hyde, it is very natural for humans to want to be the virtuous and socially acceptable Dr Jekyll, or even Edward Bernays, with his nose for opportunities but not without their opportunisms (Tye 1998).[146] It is of essence, therefore, to have an understanding and sympathy for the many and often contradictory impulses driving us as human beings (even psychoanalysts!), whether those impulses are "rational" or "irrational," or a carefully balanced or even a welter of both. Then, perhaps, we can finally see past dualisms and learn to appreciate and relate to Dr Jekyll and Mr Hyde not as two different entities, but one and the same: just like the *"Same Same but Different"* Cambodian T-shirt alluded to above.

The story about Bernays, marketing and public relations by mining and manipulating the unconscious is instructive. A case in point is the fact that Bernays could help companies sell cars and cigarettes, even though he personally neither drove a car nor smoked cigarettes (Tye 1998: 199). Equally noteworthy is the fact that the effects of any persuasive communication are not always confined to intended outcomes, nor are such outcomes always guaranteed. Take the female smokers, for instance. Bernays's intention, of course, was to help the American Tobacco Company make money and to laugh all the way to the bank himself, but who knows if he also, perhaps, with his "Torches of Freedom to protest man's inhumanity to women",[147] sowed a seed for real gender and sexual liberation that has gradually worked its way through society into maturity under the Trump era *#MeToo* movement championed by women protesting sexual harassment and the commodification and commercialisation of their bodies by men and the male dominated industries of entertainment and desire?[148] The actions of humans, including Bernays, always have consequences beyond what is intended. Even the most calculating plotter can never foresee all the consequences of his/her actions. Not addressed in this essay, but worthy of note is the question of what Bernays himself was really thinking, over and above what he has written and the interviews he has given. Maybe he, too, had a multiplicity of thoughts and intentions that do not easily yield to the logic of binary oppositions between rationality and irrationality (the elite and the masses), public relations and propaganda, and zero-sum games which he dramatised, fed upon and fed his clients in his public relations endeavours (Tye 1998).[149] In this connection, Larry Tye remarks:

But Bernays was also a bundle of contradictions. He rode roughshod over young staffers even as he ballyhooed the virtues of tolerance and democracy. He promoted cigarettes, which he suspected were deadly, at the same time he was promoting national health insurance. He espoused women's rights but often treated his female employees, and even his wife, like indentured servants. And he continually capitalized on the fact that he had outlived all his contemporaries – he died in 1995 at age 103 – to advance his contention that he, more than they, deserved to be called the prince of publicity. Although he was a small man, his claims were as huge as his dreams-and sometimes just as fanciful (Tye 1998: x).

It is in this sense that Bernays's daughter, Anne Bernays, interviewed by Adam Curtis for five hours towards *The Century of the Self* documentary, was scandalised to see that Curtis had made of her father a villain on par with Adolf Hitler. Although she herself was quite critical of her father, who in her estimation was elitist and an "awful snob" who thought little of the masses, and who believed that reality was not quite reality if not mass mediated – he once said of a stage performance by her, that "if it wasn't reviewed it didn't happen" – this did not warrant him to be qualified as a monster of Hitler-like stature, even if his writing on propaganda was a great inspiration to Joseph Goebbels, Hitler's Minister of Propaganda from 1933 to 1945 (Tye 1998: 113–139).[150] To Bernays, the elitist snob, "there was nothing better than being judged an equal by men of power and stature" (Tye 1998: 154). Put differently, it is not always that our beliefs and practices are a rational reflection of our actions, and vice versa (Tye 1998: 92–93).

The intention of any persuasive communication might be to win people over completely. It is however difficult for people to be completely reduced to unthinking consumers or hapless receptacles all the time, or even at all. People are malleable, but not infinitely so, just as they are not wholly independent and self-reliant either. They do not live their lives in splendid isolation, even in contexts where the death of society is proclaimed or desired. Even as consumers, people might not necessarily invest a product with the exact same meaning that the producers intended, especially when very deep, unconscious desires are involved. Even in totalitarian contexts of dictatorship and a personality cult where people are supposedly numbed, brainwashed and zombified, there will always be subversion and contestation of normalised conventional meanings, intentional or not, despite intended outputs, or outcomes, or both. Individuals targeted by persuasive communication "may welcome, accept or collude in some cases, but in others they may ignore, select, reshape, redirect, adapt and, on occasions, even completely reject [media content]. Even when the same material is available to all and widely consumed, the eventual outcome may vary considerably both within and between countries" (Halloran 1993: 3). Although it is possible to deeply manipulate people's minds, it is hard to be convinced that the control could ever be total. And this is what makes people like Edward Bernays and Donald Trump or the people behind entities like Cambridge Analytica (such as Steve Bannon) much less cynically one-dimensional and blinkered than they frighteningly tend to make believe. They, too, are humans, products as well as producers of society, and their powers are not unlimited, even if for purposes of salesmanship they might lay claim to unlimited power. This gives weight to the recognition and need for constant reminder that even the most obsessed, the most driven, the most rough and tough, and the most powerful are, after all is said and done, quite simply, just human.

There is reason to wonder if identities can literally be bought and sold, or if what is sold and bought is just a symbol or an expression of an identity that was always there, deeply embedded in one's layered, composite and open-ended self, à la Amos Tutuola's incompleteness of being (Nyamnjoh 2017a,

2017[2015]b). For instance, let us consider a gender category beyond the neat dichotomy emphasised by Bernays, a category that may have resulted, inadvertently from his "Torches of Freedom" public relations stunt. It is a category that muddies the waters of dichotomies, especially in terms of desires. Transgender people see themselves as men or women or transitioning from one state to the other even though they do not pass as women or men in society, and when they go for hormone treatment, surgery or whatever other form of activation, it is not to become the one or the other (which they already are in their compositeness and fluidity of being), but *to be seen* as women or men. In many cases (not including transgenderism) there might often be a dialectic involved, with consumer goods influencing identity and identity influencing consumer behaviour. As with everything, it is neither exclusively one nor the other, but an intricate comingling. Desires and aspirations are part and parcel of living in an environment along with other humans of myriad dispositions and creatures, natural and supernatural. Instead of taking human beings in their multiplicities and interconnections superficially and harnessing them simply as a means for moneymaking, access to power and privilege, our societies and their cultural, economic and political leadership would do well to look deeper and see what lies at the core of the essence of being human through relationships with others. Inclusivity, domesticated agency, conviviality or *Ubuntu-ism* and the opportunities it affords individuals and collectivities are possible even within the individualised (old and new individualism alike) human beings of the consumer society. What it takes to see, appreciate and nourish the interconnections, interdependences and openness to inclusive success is to find the humility of recognising humanity disabused of deceptively edifying but downrightly sterile and impoverishing ambitions of conquest and dominance through

93

the illusory belief in absolute victories and absolute defeats (Nyamnjoh 2015; 2017[2015]b).

Neither the individual voter, nor the politician seeking electoral success, nor the psychologist seeking to capitalise on both the individual and the politician is actually free (regardless of what they might feel), as they are all slaves to their own desires, and all co-implicated, entangled and even swallowed up in the production, reproduction and transformation of everyday relationships, desires, fears and hopes. The challenge is how to remind ourselves of the importance of being human through relationships with others, by celebrating interconnections and interdependencies in lieu of zero-sum aspirations of dichotomies and absolute victories. Seen in these terms, one is bound to ask whether seeking to radically oppose between or put asunder rationality and irrationality, the elite and the masses, the individual and the group is the best way of living together in a world of ever-new desires and aspirations? Is there no better way of being than through absolute autonomy and absolute victories? Is it really that hurtful to be autonomous and victorious together, not only with other individuals, but with the environment along with the other creatures, big and small, tangible and intangible, with whom we share our lives and our planet without always being aware of their existence?

Endnotes

[1] See https://www.youtube.com/watch?v=eJ3RzGoQC4s&t=13s, accessed 30 March 2018.

[2] Which basically makes money by monitoring and monetising the privacy of its users. Its clients such as Cambridge Analytica then use the facts gathered from the browsing histories of its users to create a web of disinformation online, inviting those entrapped to click on things that make them think things are happening, when it is actually an invitation to live in a truthless (post-truth or post-consensus) world, available and amenable to being manipulated ad infinitum by the hidden persuaders who control the algorithms that make that world possible. This is evidence not only of the manipulability of social media, but also of the fact that the cheap and affordable delivery of goods and services made possible by social media come at great costs to privacy and individual freedoms. Granted that Facebook has brought millions of people around the world together and also that consumers have tended to blindly surrender the facts of their lives in the excitement of connectivity made possible, what role must Facebook and other social media platforms play in protecting democracy from opportunism? Is it enough to simply claim that social media are connecting the world and should therefore be celebrated for doing so, when the prospects of their misappropriation and weaponisation are so glaring (Nance 2018; Watts 2018)? The UK parliamentary Digital, Culture, Media and Sport (DCMS) Committee set up to investigate disinformation and fake news following the Cambridge Analytica data scandal, does not think so. The committee calls on closer regulation of social media, arguing that "Social media companies cannot hide behind the claim of being merely a 'platform', claiming that they are tech companies and have no role themselves in regulating the content of their sites". See BBC, "Fake news a democratic crisis, MPs warn", https://www.bbc.com/news/technology-44967650, accessed 28 July 2018.'

[3] Steve Bannon, who describes himself as a populist and a nationalist at heart, served as Donald Trump's campaign manager during the 2016 presidential election (Green 2017; Koffler 2017), was said to like to have an exalted opinion of himself as the puppet master behind the scenes, the evil genius who wanted to be recognised as the mind behind Donald Trump's electoral success (Wolff 2018). See also, "Steve Bannon CNN Full Interview with Fareed Zakaria", https://youtu.be/4rCUZShbp0s, accessed 5 June 2018, and "Steve Bannon extended interview on Europe's far-right and Cambridge Analytica", https://youtu.be/pold15c8H70, accessed 9 June 2018. According to whistleblower Christopher Wylie, Bannon reportedly

wanted the services of Cambridge Analytica's expertise in psychological profiling to wage a culture war that included suppressing, discouraging or demobilising voting by certain individuals and social categories (African-Americans in particular) most likely to vote Democrat and/or against Republican. See Donie O'Sullivan and Drew Griffin, "Cambridge Analytica ran voter suppression campaigns, whistleblower claims", https://amp.cnn.com/cnn/2018/05/16/politics/cambridge-analytica-congress-wylie/index.html, accessed 17 May 2018.

[4] See Carole Cadwalladr and Emma Graham-Harrison, "Revealed: 50 million Facebook profiles harvested for Cambridge Analytica in major data breach", https://www.theguardian.com/news/2018/mar/17/cambridge-analytica-facebook-influence-us-election; and Matthew Rosenberg, Nicholas Confessore and Carole Cadwalladr, "How Trump Consultants Exploited the Facebook Data of Millions", https://www.nytimes.com/2018/03/17/us/politics/cambridge-analytica-trump-campaign.html, accessed 23 March 2018. See also "Facebook Says Data Leak Hits 87 Million Users, Widening Privacy Scandal", http://ewn.co.za/2018/04/05/facebook-says-data-leak-hits-87-million-users-widening-privacy-scandal, accessed 8 April 2018; and http://www.bbc.com/news/av/technology-43674480/facebook-data-how-it-was-used-by-cambridge-analytica, accessed 9 April 2018. See also, *The Rachel Maddow Show* on MSNBC, "New Cambridge Analytica Revelations Connect President Trump Russia Dots", https://youtu.be/VAyBJLA2syg, accessed 7 June 2018.

[5] See Casey Newton, "Mark Zuckerberg apologizes for the Cambridge Analytica scandal", https://www.theverge.com/2018/3/21/17150158/mark-zuckerberg-cnn-interview-cambridge-analytica, accessed 23 March 2018.

[6] Jina Moore, "Cambridge Analytica Had a Role in Kenya Election, Too", https://www.nytimes.com/2018/03/20/world/africa/kenya-cambridge-analytica-election.html, accessed 30 March 2018.

[7] See "Cambridge Analytica whistleblower Christopher Wylie appears before MPs – watch live", https://www.youtube.com/watch?v=X5g6IJm7YJQ, accessed 6 June 2018.

[8] The statement issued by Cambridge Analytica announcing its shutdown, read:

> Over the past several months, Cambridge Analytica has been the subject of numerous unfounded accusations and, despite the company's efforts to correct the record, has been vilified for activities that are not only legal, but also widely accepted as a standard component of online advertising in both the political and commercial arenas. Despite Cambridge Analytica's unwavering confidence that its employees have acted ethically and lawfully ...

the siege of media coverage has driven away virtually all of the company's customers and suppliers. As a result, it has been determined that it is no longer viable to continue operating the business. See "Cambridge Analytica: Facebook data-harvest firm to shut", http://www.bbc.com/news/business-43983958, accessed 3 May 2018.

[9] Indeed, Cyberpace is increasingly so much of a battleground that former President Bill Clinton felt motivated enough to co-author a novel with James Patterson that revolves around cyber terror, espionage, criminality and treason deserving of the single-minded attention and whole-hearted patriotism of the president to save a nation paralysed by fear and uncertainty (Clinton and Patterson 2018). To listen to the authors talk about the book and related matters in Trump's America, see also, "Bill Clinton & James Patterson – 'The President Is Missing' | *The Daily Show*", https://youtu.be/wKjr0Z8FulE, accessed 9 July 2018.

[10] See BBC, "Fake news a democratic crisis, MPs warn", https://www.bbc.com/news/technology-44967650, accessed 28 July 2018.

[11] See "The Barack Obama 2018 Nelson Mandela lecture", https://mg.co.za/article/2018-07-18-read-in-full-the-barack-obama-2018-nelson-mandela-lecture, accessed 24 July 2018.

[12] See *The Century of the Self*, Part 4: "Eight People Sipping Wine in Kettering", https://www.youtube.com/watch?v=VouaAz5mQAs, accessed 13 March 2018.

[13] This is what David Pecker of the *National Enquirer*, a tabloid own by American Media, reportedly did to conceal extramarital affairs by Donald Trump. Women whose stories were bought and killed included Karen McDougal, a former Playboy model, and Stormy Daniels, a pornstar (see Brian Stelter, "'Catch and kill': How a tabloid shields Trump from troublesome stories", https://money.cnn.com/2018/02/16/media/trump-catch-and-kill/index.html, accessed 26 July 2018). An excerpt of a report on the Karen McDougal story reads: "The company that owns the National Enquirer [American Media], a backer of Donald Trump, agreed to pay $150,000 to a former Playboy centerfold model for her story of an affair a decade ago with the Republican presidential nominee, but then didn't publish it" (see Joe Palazzolo, Michael Rothfeld and Lukas I. Alpert, "National Enquirer Shielded Donald Trump From Playboy Model's Affair Allegation: Tabloid owner American Media agreed to pay $150,000 for story from 1998 Playmate of the Year, but hasn't published her account", https://www.wsj.com/articles/national-enquirer-shielded-donald-trump-from-playboy-models-affair-allegation-1478309380, accessed 26 July 2018). The report was eventually authenticated by a secretly recorded conversation with Trump by his personal lawyer, Michael Cohen, made available to CNN in July 2018 (see Chris Cuomo, Kara Scannell and Eli Watkins, "Exclusive: CNN obtains secret Trump-Cohen tape", https://edition.cnn.com/2018/07/24/politics/michael-cohen-donald-

trump-tape/index.html, accessed 26 July 2018; see also *The Last Word with Lawrence O'Donnell*, "More Michael Cohen Tapes Coming? Michael Cohen 'Kicks Back' At Donald Trump, MSNBC'', https://youtu.be/WvYkoJyidUc, accessed 26 July 2018; and see also, CNN, "Breaking News Trump 7/27/18 Michael Cohen Is Prepared To Tell Mueller Donald Trump Knew, and Approved of, Trump Tower Meeting Before it Happened", https://youtu.be/mKB10vFTQ7Q, accessed 27 July 2018).

[14] This theme is the subject of an enriching conversation in Sylvie Rokab's 2015 documentary film, "Love Thy Nature", on the need to question the human tendency to arrogate to ourselves the status of being the most intelligent, self-reflexive and wise of the world's creatures, and through such reasoning, to assume that the rest of the natural environment is ours to manipulate, appropriate and harness to suit our every whim and caprice as the only *truly rational* beings, and by extension, the only creatures who *truly feel* in ways that matter or should matter (See https://www.lovethynature.com/, accessed 15 July 2018). Such reasoning that dramatises the superiority of humans encourages a mentality of borrowing without acknowledgement and harvesting without replenishing, and fails to recognise the need for human interaction and interdependence with fellow humans, the natural environment and the supernatural world informed by a reality of intricate and multidimensional interconnections (Nyamnjoh 2017a).

[15] In this connection, Allen Frances (2013) is very critical of the tendency in American medical psychiatric practice to prescribe anti-depressants in lieu of genuinely taking time to understand the real causes of the aches and pains of everyday life for millions of Americans desperately seeking solace. He argues that such quick prescriptions and trigger-happy approach to medication put people at risk of side effects such as weight gain, low sex drive and diminishing pride in their own resiliency as individuals and social beings. "Unsane", a 2018 film directed by Steven Soderbergh, also speaks to this practice and concern. In the film, "Sawyer Valentini relocates from Boston to Pennsylvania to escape from the man who's been stalking her for the last two years. While consulting with a therapist, Valentini unwittingly signs in for a voluntary 24-hour commitment to the Highland Creek Behavioral Center". She is administered anti-depressants as her word and sanity are questioned, a reaction that results in violent outbursts and protests that are seen by the doctors and nurses as evidence of her insanity. See https://en.wikipedia.org/wiki/Unsane (film), accessed 15 July 2018; See also https://www.imdb.com/title/tt7153766/, accessed 15 July 2018.

[16] After an 8 June 1982 speech in the British House of Commons in which Ronald Reagan argued that freedom is not the sole prerogative of a limited few, and called for the creation of institutions to foster the infrastructure of democracy globally, his government went on to create a state-funded

National Endowment for Democracy, with the National Democratic Institute and the National Republican Institute as its Democratic and Republican parties offshoots. See *"The Rachel Maddow Show 6/9/18"*, https://www.youtube.com/watch?v=5kfVvq924Nw, accessed 9 June 2018. See also "Address to Members of the British Parliament June 8, 1982", https://www.reaganlibrary.gov/sites/default/files/archives/speeches/1982/60882a.htm, accessed 9 June 2018.

[17] It remains to be seen the extent to which the election of Donald Trump actually challenges this, and for how long. Could his valorisation and capitalisation of the restless white American masses of his Republican Party only serve to produce and unify the restless Black, Latino and Muslim American masses whom he repeatedly attacks and disparages in his incendiary red-meat rhetoric fed his hard core red-meat supporters at his red-meat rallies?

[18] See also "Edward Bernays: the Father of Spin – Larry Tye Book Interview (1998)", https://www.youtube.com/watch?v=lQgMxKQ7mX8, accessed 9 June 2018.

[19] See also "Edward Bernays: the Father of Spin – Larry Tye Book Interview (1998)", https://www.youtube.com/watch?v=lQgMxKQ7mX8, accessed 9 June 2018; see also "Mark Crispin Miller & Anne Bernays, Edward Bernays' *Propaganda*", https://www.youtube.com/watch?v=4ZBDDUNdXyU, accessed 9 June 2018.

[20] See Richard Gunderman, "The manipulation of the American mind: Edward Bernays and the birth of public relations", https://theconversation.com/the-manipulation-of-the-american-mind-edward-bernays-and-the-birth-of-public-relations-44393, accessed 11 April 2018. See also "Edward Bernays, 'Father of Public Relations' And Leader in Opinion Making, Dies at 103", https://archive.nytimes.com/www.nytimes.com/books/98/08/16/specials/bernays-obit.html?_r=1, accessed 11 April 2018.

[21] See Ronald Blumer, "The Invention of Public Relations", https://www.youtube.com/watch?v=iBEclayBCdc&feature=youtu.be, accessed 16 April 2018; see also "Edward Bernays: the Father of Spin – Larry Tye Book Interview (1998)", https://www.youtube.com/watch?v=lQgMxKQ7mX8, accessed 9 June 2018.

[22] See Gary H. Grossman, Rob Blumenstein, and Sean P Geary, "Sell & Spin: A History of Advertising", https://www.youtube.com/watch?v=YPBf7km7NAk&t=890s, accessed 12 May 2018. See also, "Consumerism", https://www.youtube.com/watch?v=8l5fRI-YnG0&feature=youtu.be, accessed 27 May 2018.

23 See *The Century of the Self*, Part 1: "The Happiness Machines", https://www.youtube.com/watch?v=DnPmg0R1M04, accessed 13 February 2018.

24 See Ronald Blumer, "The Invention of Public Relations", https://www.youtube.com/watch?v=iBEclayBCdc&feature=youtu.be, accessed 16 April 2018. The parallels are remarkable between Wilson's liberator, champion of the people and creator of a new world of freedom propaganda by the Committee on Public Information, and Donald Trump's action movie-like video produced by Destiny Pictures in preparation for his "denuclearisation summit" with Kim Jong Un of North Korea, which took place on 12 June 2018 in Singapore. The said video invited Kim Jong Un to "shake the hand of peace" offered by Donald Trump and be part of the remaking of history and the writing of a new future of riches and material superabundance for his people and for himself. See "The action-movie style trailer Trump says he played to Kim Jong-un", https://youtu.be/aYsaC2CADs0, accessed 14 June 2018.

25 See "Subconscious Fascism – Edward Bernays", https://www.youtube.com/watch?v=ZZNHhzOj3o0, accessed 17 April 2018; see also, "Mark Crispin Miller & Anne Bernays, Edward Bernays' *Propaganda*", https://www.youtube.com/watch?v=4ZBDDUNdXyU, accessed 9 June 2018.

26 See Ronald Blumer, "The Invention of Public Relations", https://www.youtube.com/watch?v=iBEclayBCdc&feature=youtu.be, accessed 16 April 2018; "Subconscious Fascism – Edward Bernays", https://www.youtube.com/watch?v=ZZNHhzOj3o0, accessed 17 April 2018.

27 Again, note the early importance of individual and collective psychology as well as the interplay of rational and irrational elements in social change campaigns.

28 See *The Century of the Self*, Part 1: "The Happiness Machines", https://www.youtube.com/watch?v=DnPmg0R1M04, accessed 13 February 2018; "Feminism and Propaganda: Torches of Freedom", https://www.youtube.com/watch?v=Ljj6H3B3oAs; and "How smoking became a symbol of the 'Emancipated Woman'", https://www.youtube.com/watch?v=ovBRPVQJ9EI, accessed 11 April 2018; see also James Corbett, "Meet Edward Bernays, Master of Propaganda", https://www.youtube.com/watch?v=44I3pMouCnM&t=924s, accessed 17 April 2018; see also, "Edward Bernays: the Father of Spin – Larry Tye Book Interview (1998)", https://www.youtube.com/watch?v=lQgMxKQ7mX8, accessed 9 June 2018.

29 See Ronald Blumer, "The Invention of Public Relations", https://www.youtube.com/watch?v=iBEclayBCdc&feature=youtu.be,

accessed 16 April 2018; "Subconscious Fascism – Edward Bernays", https://www.youtube.com/watch?v=ZZNHhzOj3o0, accessed 17 April 2018.

[30] It is also possible, to argue that women perceived smoking as the symbolic, albeit misguided, dimension of a rational struggle for sex equality.

[31] See "Edward Bernays – The Ultimate Propagandist – National History Day 2009", https://www.youtube.com/watch?v=K7vPiA3HyWQ&feature=youtu.be, accessed 13 April 2018.

[32] See "Consumerism", https://www.youtube.com/watch?v=8l5fRI-YnG0&feature=youtu.be, accessed 27 May 2018.

[33] See Gary H. Grossman, Rob Blumenstein and Sean P Geary, "Sell & Spin: A History of Advertising", https://www.youtube.com/watch?v=YPBf7km7NAk&t=890s, accessed 12 May 2018.

[34] See *The Century of the Self*, Part 2: "The Engineering of Consent", https://www.youtube.com/watch?v=fEsPOt8MG7E, accessed 13 March 2018.

[35] See Friedrick A. Hayek, 1961, "The Non Sequitur of the 'Dependence Effect'", https://bastiat.mises.org/sites/default/files/The%20Non%20Sequitur%20of%20the%20Dependence%20Effect_4.pdf, accessed 2 May 2018.

[36] See Gary H. Grossman, Rob Blumenstein and Sean P Geary, "Sell & Spin: A History of Advertising", https://www.youtube.com/watch?v=YPBf7km7NAk&t=890s, accessed 12 May 2018; see also, "Consumerism", https://www.youtube.com/watch?v=8l5fRI-YnG0&feature=youtu.be, accessed 27 May 2018.

[37] See "Consumerism", https://www.youtube.com/watch?v=8l5fRI-YnG0&feature=youtu.be, accessed 27 May 2018.

[38] See "Consumerism", https://www.youtube.com/watch?v=8l5fRI-YnG0&feature=youtu.be, accessed 27 May 2018.

[39] Bernays personally engineered many such newsworthy campaigns, which Larry Tye discusses in detail in his book, *The Father of Spin: Edward L. Bernays and the Birth of Public Relations* (1998), including the demonisation campaign he designed and led against Guatemala's socialist leader Jacobo Arbenz Guzman – a campaign in which "the U.S. public was made to believe it was fighting against tyranny", although the "real beneficiary of that get-tough policy" was the "United Fruit Company, whose banana republic was threatened by Guatemala's new leftist government" (Tye 1998: vi–viii; 155–184). Another good example of how Bernays's manipulation of symbols had caught on and became normalised in the USA was the carefully engineered 2 August 1990–28 February 1991 Persian Gulf War, by an American Public

Relations firm, "Hill and Knowlton, in a campaign bought and paid for by rich Kuwaitis who were Saddam [Hussein]'s archenemies". This was a war against Saddam Hussein's Iraq by a Western coalition led by President George H. W. Bush of the USA. As Larry Tye observes in the preface to his biography on Edward Bernays, "the whole notion that the United States had been rallied to war by a massive hidden PR campaign left many Americans doubting the soundness of their own opinions and wondering whether our very thoughts were being tampered with right here in the hub of democracy" (Tye 1998: vii).

[40] See Ronald Blumer, "The Invention of Public Relations", https://www.youtube.com/watch?v=iBEclayBCdc&feature=youtu.be, accessed 16 April 2018.

[41] See Steve Schmidt, "By A fluke, Voters Elected an Imbecilic Con Man", *Morning Joe*, MSNBC, https://youtu.be/mLDKdoOZsGM, accessed 26 June 2018. In an interview with Chris Hayes, Steve Schmidt explains his decision to quit the Republican Party over Trump immigration policy, calling Trump an autocrat and a danger to American liberal democracy. See *"All In with Chris Hayes 6/26/2018 | MSNBC NEWS* June 26, 2018", https://youtu.be/S8HJh8Vyowk, accessed 27 June 2018. George F. Will, a Republican and former Fox News contributor, called Republicans in Congress as Trump's "poodles", urging Republicans to vote against them at the 2018 November mid-term elections. See Douglas Ernst, "George Will demands voters punish 'king' Trump's Republican 'poodles'", https://www.washingtontimes.com/news/2018/jun/22/george-will-demands-voters-punish-king-trumps-repu/, accessed 27 June 2018.

[42] This is a famous expression by Donald Trump in his book, *The Art of the Deal*, co-authored with Tony Schwartz (who repeatedly insists in his TV interviews that Trump can neither read nor write, and that Trump did not as much as write a word of the book), in which Trump says:

> The final key to the way I promote is bravado. I play to people's fantasies. People may not always think big themselves, but they can still get very excited by those who do. That's why a little hyperbole never hurts. People want to believe that something is the biggest and the greatest and the most spectacular.
>
> I call it truthful hyperbole. It's an innocent form of exaggeration – and a very effective form of promotion (Trump with Schwartz 1987: 58). See also, "Tony Schwartz: The Truth about Trump | Oxford Union Q&A", https://youtu.be/qxF_CDDJ0YI, accessed 18 June 2018.

Trump's penchant for exaggeration is remarkably similar to that of Edward Bernays, who according to Larry Tye:

> … couldn't recount an old PR campaign without insisting it was precedent-setting, and he couldn't eat a simple bowl of fish soup

without pronouncing it "the best fish soup ever". His family knew that exaggeration was an element of his work that long ago had become an element of his personality. They also knew their grandfather really believed the soup was the best, which made it easier for them to accept his hyperbole (Tye 1998: 207).

Back to Trump, little wonder that in their war of words when North Korean leader, Kim Jong-Un claimed his nuclear button was on his desk at all times, Trump could not resist the temptation of size when he retorted in a tweet:

> North Korean Leader Kim Jong Un just stated that the "Nuclear Button is on his desk at all times". Will someone from his depleted and food starved regime please inform him that I too have a Nuclear Button, but it is a much bigger & more powerful one than his, and my Button works! (See, "'Mine is bigger than yours': Trump to North Korea about his nuclear button", https://www.timeslive.co.za/news/world/2018-01-03-mine-is-bigger-than-yours-trump-to-north-korea-about-his-nuclear-button/, accessed 30 May 2018.

Such disturbing exchange of boastful insults notwithstanding (Gartner et al. 2018), Trump, in a surprising about-turn, agreed/offered to meet Kim Jong Un in a summit that took place in Singapore on 12 June 2018. The summit was widely thought to have resulted in greater diplomatic victory for the North Korean leader than for Trump, who, despite his claims to the contrary, reportedly promised much without a clear commitment in the signed declaration from Kim Jong Un on the unconditional, verifiable denuclearisation that his administration is supposed to have sought. See Stephen Collinson, "Lingering questions from the Trump-Kim summit", https://edition.cnn.com/2018/06/12/politics/what-really-came-out-of-the-trump-kim-summit/index.html, accessed 14 June 2018. See also E.J. Dionne Jr, "There's no defending Trump's North Korea performance", https://www.washingtonpost.com/opinions/trumps-north-korean-fantasyland/2018/06/13/0f9614a8-6f44-11e8-afd5-778aca903bbe_story.html?noredirect=on&utm_term=.96c28bef4a16, accessed 14 June 2018.

43 According to David Ignatius, beyond his "braggadocio", Trump is a "scarred, prickly and needy" person who "picks needless fights and tries to humiliate people he feels have slighted him". As president, Trump projects the "core pessimism" and "bleak vision" that have come to characterise him (his art of deal notwithstanding) onto America (contrary to its normal "idealistic, generous national self-image"), which he sees "as exhausted, played out, bled financially by its allies and manipulated by its trading partners". See "Trump is scarred, prickly and needy", https://www.washingtonpost.com/opinions/trumps-neediness-is-at-the-

core-of-his-diplomacy/2018/07/10/b153f844-8477-11e8-8553-a3ce89036c78_story.html?noredirect=on&utm_term=.e005ce921458, accessed 12 July 2018. See also "Donald Trump REALLY POWERFUL Full Documentary 2016", https://youtu.be/Ng3LjuUgxwc, accessed 11 June 2018.

[44] See Steve Schmidt, "By A fluke, Voters Elected an Imbecilic Con Man," *Morning Joe*, MSNBC, https://youtu.be/mLDKdoOZsGM, accessed 26 June 2018.

[45] According to George Will, "Precision is not part of Trump's repertoire: He speaks English as though it is a second language that he learned from someone who learned English last week. So, it is usually difficult to sift meanings from Trump's word salads." See https://www.washingtonpost.com/opinions/this-sad-embarrassing-wreck-of-a-man/2018/07/17/d06de8ea-89e8-11e8-a345-a1bf7847b375_story.html?utm_term=.e35b4c4ae769, accessed 19 July 2018.

[46] See "Jon Stewart Is Ready to Negotiate with Donald Trump", https://youtu.be/PYCPZrOkZx0, accessed 29 June 2018.

[47] According to his former adviser, Sebastian Gorka, Trump has 53 million followers on Twitter, whom, as the master communicator that he is, Trump targets to with his messages to good effect. See Channel 4 News, "Former Trump adviser Sebastian Gorka lauds the President's UK visit", https://youtu.be/8AjsGxmxBOk, accessed 15 July 2018.

[48] See *The Beat with Ari Melber* 6/23/18 | BREAKING NEWS WEEKEND June 23, 2018| MSNBC", https://youtu.be/sjSOJw33aik, accessed 24 June 2018.

[49] In an effort to speak increasingly to his base only, using media that he can manipulate in the manner that former President Richard Nixon had only dreamt about, in July 2018 Trump hired former Fox News co-president, Bill Shine as deputy chief of staff for communication. See "Trump Taps Controversial Ex-Fox Executive for Key White House Job | *The Beat with Ari Melber* | "SNBC, https://youtu.be/R0Z-lKauBok", accessed 6 July 2018. See also *The Rachel Maddow Show* 07/05/18 | Breaking News Trump [Full]" on YouTube, https://youtu.be/Yc4yKpsLYiY, accessed 6 July 2018.

[50] See Katie Rogers and Maggie Haberman, "Spotting CNN on a TV aboard Air Force One, Trump Rages against Reality", https://www.nytimes.com/2018/07/24/us/politics/trump-putin-cnn.html, accessed 26 July 2018. On a second case in point, CNN reporter Kaitlan Collins was disinvited by press secretary Sarah Huckabee Sanders and communications director Bill Shine "from a late-afternoon announcement in the Rose Garden involving Trump and European Commission President Jean-Claude Juncker a few hours after she sought to question Trump during a press-pool 'spray' in the Oval Office". Following widespread criticism of the ban, the White House issued the following statement: "At the conclusion of a press event in the Oval Office a reporter shouted questions and refused to leave despite repeatedly being asked to do so. Subsequently,

our staff informed her she was not welcome to participate in the next event, but made clear that any other journalist from her network could attend. She said it didn't matter to her because she hadn't planned to be there anyway. To be clear, we support a free press and ask that everyone be respectful of the presidency and guests at the White House" (see Paul Farhi and Felicia Sonmez, "CNN reporter barred from White House event, drawing protests from journalists", https://www.washingtonpost.com/lifestyle/style/cnn-reporter-barred-from-white-house-event-drawing-journalists-protests/2018/07/25/81dd6b5e-9057-11e8-bcd5-9d911c784c38_story.html?utm_term=.3cfd461c1f65, accessed 26 July 2018).

[51] An excerpt of the blurb of *The Daily Show* with Trevor Noah and Jon Meacham 2018 book reads:

> Comprising hundreds of Trump tweets, and featuring a foreword by Pulitzer Prize-winning historian Jon Meacham, and even a place for readers to add their own future Trump tweet highlights – because he is making new Twitter history literally every day – The Donald J. Trump Presidential Twitter Library is a unique portrait of an artist whose masterworks will be studied by historians, grammarians, and mental health professionals for years to come.

[52] According to *The Guardian*, a Cambridge Analytica employee "had 'reached out' to Assange in July 2016 and offered to help him index and distribute the 33,000 emails that had been stolen from Hillary Clinton". A director of Cambridge Analytica, Brittany Kaiser, reportedly visited Julius Assange of WikiLeaks and "claimed to have channelled cryptocurrency payments and donations to WikiLeaks". See "Cambridge Analytica director 'met Assange to discuss US election'", https://www.theguardian.com/uk-news/2018/jun/06/cambridge-analytica-brittany-kaiser-julian-assange-wikileaks, accessed 8 June 2018.

[53] See Rachel Maddow on MSNBC, "New Cambridge Analytica Revelations Connect President Trump Russia Dots", https://youtu.be/VAyBJLA2syg, accessed 7 June 2018.

[54] It should be added, however, that when relations eventually soured between the two, following publication by Michael Wolff of *Fire and Fury: Inside the Trump White House* (2018), a book mostly credited to insights from Steve Bannon, Trump issued a statement minimising the role Bannon played in his campaign and victory. Parts of the statement read:

> "Steve had very little to do with our historic victory, which was delivered by the forgotten men and women of this country", Trump said. "Yet Steve had everything to do with the loss of a Senate seat in Alabama held for more than thirty years by Republicans. Steve doesn't represent my base -- he's only in it for himself". "Steve pretends to be at war with the media, which he

calls the opposition party, yet he spent his time at the White House leaking false information to the media to make himself seem far more important than he was", Trump said. "It is the only thing he does well. Steve was rarely in a one-on-one meeting with me and only pretends to have had influence to fool a few people with no access and no clue, whom he helped write phony books". See Alex Wayne and Jennifer Jacobs, "Trump Says Bannon 'Lost His Mind' After Leaving White House", https://www.bloomberg.com/news/articles/2018-01-03/trump-says-bannon-lost-his-mind-after-leaving-white-house, accessed 3 January 2018.

Bannon had committed the unpardonable offence of yielding to the temptation of caprice by thinking of himself as more worthy of praise. For claiming the status of being the brain and genius behind the "really smart" and "stable genius" of a president, Bannon found himself stripped of such pretensions in broad daylight, humbled and humiliated by the power of the president's wallet and his uncanny ability to control the wallets of many other rich, privileged and powerful men and women. In Trump's Reality TV world of hire and fire, building up suspense and then a big reveal, there is only one boss (however capricious and impulsive), as everyone else is reduced to a mere apprentice, whatever their genius and whatever their talent. He does not have the habit or the experience of taking a position against himself. Even when the chips are not down and his interests not at stake, he is reportedly there to hurt and not to help. Rick Wilson's book title in this regard reads *Every Thing Trump Touches Dies* (2018). With him, it would appear there is no such thing, beyond rhetoric, as just wanting to make the world a better place.

55 Even when pushed by overwhelming public outrage – as happened during the Charlottesville protests, the separation of children from their parents as part of the zero tolerance immigration policy, or after the Helsinki meeting with Putin – Trump walks back only to walk back the walk back, and unsays things only to say them again.

56 During the 2016 Presidential election, Trump insisted he would only accept the results of the election, if he was the winner:

"Ladies and gentleman, I want to make a major announcement today", he said at a rally at the Delaware County Fair in Ohio. "I would like to promise and pledge to all of my voters and supporters and to all of the people of the United States that I will totally accept the results of this great and historic presidential election if I win". See Christine Wang, "Trump: I will 'totally accept' the results of this election 'if I win'", https://www.cnbc.com/2016/10/20/trump-i-will-totally-accept-the-results-of-this-election-if-i-win.html, accessed 9 June 2018.

[57] With reference to African, Haitian and Latino immigrants, during an immigration agenda-setting meeting at the White House, Trump reportedly slurred: "Why are we having all these people from shithole countries come here?" Pointedly at Haitians, a people he has singled out to summarily condemn as all infected and afflicted by AIDS, he is said to have been particularly infuriated: "Why do we need more Haitians? Take them out", he instructed, adding that if he had his way, more immigrants should be attracted from Europe, especially from the Scandinavian countries such as Norway (see "President Trump Called El Salvador, Haiti 'Shithole Countries': Report," http://time.com/5100058/donald-trump-shithole-countries/?xid=homepage, accessed 29 May 2018). Apparently, when his parents were reluctant to identify with their German ancestry, they reportedly tested the waters of passing for Scandinavians. Is this really what is at the heart of his campaign slogan: "Make America Great Again"? The slogan is reportedly code for "Make America White Again"– the purity of whiteness that is increasingly in short supply, only to be found in European reserves such as Norway, and among the Republican whites of the USA, his unchanging and unyielding base? If there is little or no room for Blacks, Browns, LGBTQ, Muslims and Jews (even as his son-in-law is a Jew and his rhetoric at times might suggest a measure of condemnation of anti-Semitism) in such a carefully distilled idea and ideal of being American and being great again, what does the future hold for the mobile shitholes of the world? If White lives matter to Trump as president, why should this cancel out the fact that Black and Brown lives matter as well – especially, some would add, given past and present inequalities and injustices? What democracy is possible with a president who seeks legitimacy only among 1/3 of the nationals and citizens of the country he leads? What are the merits of a leader without a sense of the history of mobility of persons, ideas and ideals that has gone into the making of the unity in diversity of being American which he is called upon to protect, preserve and enrich with visionary creativity, imagination and unrelenting open-mindedness? Those inclined to a more inclusive America must feel truly demotivated when, despite President Trump's public statements of dislike and distaste for Muslims, the Supreme Court decided by a vote of 5 to 4 to uphold as constitutional the 3rd version of Trump's Travel Ban. The Trump policy applies to travellers from five countries with overwhelmingly Muslim populations – Iran, Libya, Somalia, Syria and Yemen. It also affects two non-Muslim countries, North Korea and some Venezuelan government officials and their families. This decision came despite the acknowledgement by 'Chief Justice Roberts ... that Mr. Trump had made many statements concerning his desire to impose a "Muslim ban". He recounted the president's call for a "total and complete shutdown of Muslims entering the United States", and he noted that the president has said that "Islam hates

us" and has asserted that the United States was "having problems with Muslims coming into the country". See Adam Liptak and Michael D. Shear, "Trump's Travel Ban Is Upheld by Supreme", https://www.nytimes.com/2018/06/26/us/politics/supreme-court-trump-travel-ban.html, accessed 27 June 2018. Justice Sonia Sotomayor, one of the four who dissented (the others being Justices Stephen Breyer, Ruth Bader Ginsburg and Elena Kagan), said "History will not look kindly on the court's misguided decision today, nor should it", adding that "a reasonable observer would conclude that the Proclamation was motivated by anti-Muslim animus". According to her, the majority of judges had reached their judgement by "ignoring the facts, misconstruing our legal precedent and turning a blind eye to the pain and suffering the Proclamation inflicts upon countless families and individuals, many of whom are United States citizens". See Mark Sherman, "Supreme Court upholds Trump ban on travel from several mostly Muslim countries", http://www.chicagotribune.com/news/nationworld/ct-supreme-court-trump-travel-ban-20180626-story.html, accessed 27 June 2018. See also *The Rachel Maddow Show 6/26/2018 | MSNBC NEWS June 26, 2018*", https://youtu.be/9BNJyv27-6k, accessed 27 June 2018.

[58] See "Trump Defends 'Animals' Remark, Saying It Referred to MS-13 Gang Members", https://www.nytimes.com/2018/05/17/us/trump-animals-ms-13-gangs.html, accessed 30 May 2018.

[59] In this connection, in addition to Steve Bannon, Trump's hardliner immigration adviser is Stephen Miller, who champions white nationalism in the US. See William D. Cohan, "How Stephen Miller Rode White Rage from Duke's Campus to Trump's West Wing", https://www.vanityfair.com/news/2017/05/stephen-miller-duke-donald-trump, accessed 20 June 2018. See also Cale Guthrie Weissman, "NYT under fire for spiking a Stephen Miller interview from its podcast", https://www.fastcompany.com/40586928/nyt-under-fire-for-spiking-a-stephen-miller-interview-from-its-podcast, accessed 20 June 2018.

[60] See Jennifer Rubin, "About the 'deplorables'...", https://www.washingtonpost.com/blogs/right-turn/wp/2017/08/17/about-the-deplorables/?utm_term=.32d08cf6d5da, accessed 19 June 2018.

[61] See *The Last Word with Lawrence O'Donnell*, "Breaking News Tonight Trump 6/18/18 | The Untouchables", https://youtu.be/N_d1TpkreQw, accessed 19 June 2018.

[62] See *The 11th Hour with Brian Williams*, "Breaking News Tonight Trump 6/18/18 | Trump, Muller, The White House", https://youtu.be/UKsDJOfHsT4, accessed 19 June 2018. See also a defence of the policy by Attorney General Jeff Sessions, "Breaking News

Morning Trump 6/19/18 | Trump Takes on Mueller in New Tweet",
https://youtu.be/0T4OcLplKQ8, accessed 19 June 2018.

[63] See "GOP and White House Know Something Has Gone Wrong,"
Morning Joe, MSNBC, https://youtu.be/E3V48o7IGUo, accessed 22 June
2018.

[64] See *The Last Word with Lawrence O'Donnell*, "Breaking News Tonight
Trump 6/19/18 | Trump Admin Housing Hundreds of Babies",
https://youtu.be/YyPaWMYA6CQ, accessed 20 June 2018. See also "*The
Rachel Maddow Show* June 19, 2018 | MSNBC Today 6/19/2018",
https://youtu.be/5FS6bndcEho, accessed 20 June 2018.

[65] See *The Rachel Maddow Show*, "Breaking News | Tonight 6/20/18 | Doj
Asks Pentagon to Send Military Lawyers to Border",
https://youtu.be/RfA4k1kF_Mc, accessed 21 June 2018. See also "*The Last
Word with Lawrence O'Donnell* 6/20/2018 | MSNBC NEWS June 20, 2018",
https://youtu.be/c98c1HNoT-o, on how Trump, a person who likes to
think of himself as never backing down, caved on this matter, accessed 21
June 2018. For a detailed, critical commentary on the executive order, and
especially Trump's silence on reuniting children already separated from
parents, see "*All In with Chris Hayes* June 20, 2018 | MSNBC Today
6/20/2018", https://youtu.be/de81v3c6aIw, accessed 21 June 2018. As
Rachel Maddow reported, there was little indication of procedures or plans
in place or paperwork connecting kids to parents indicative of an intention
to reunite parents and children. See "*The Rachel Maddow Show* June 21, 2018
| MSNBC Today 6/21/2018", https://youtu.be/z9E2S8_5S-4, accessed 22
June 2018. Subsequently, it was reported that the number of children
separated from their parents was about 1,768 children more than initially
reported, because the Trump administration had run pilot separation
projects for several months before the first formal implementation of the
policy. See "*The Rachel Maddow Show* 6/29/2018 | MSNBC NEWS June 29,
2018", https://youtu.be/3vY4wp0cXu8, accessed 30 June 2018.

[66] See Karl Vick, "A Reckoning after Trump's Border Separation Policy:
What Kind of Country Are We?", http://time.com/5318229/donald-
trump-border-separation-policy/, accessed 22 June 2018. The crying two-
year-old girl was captured in a photo by Pulitzer Prize-winning
photographer John Moore from Getty Images. The photo, which went
viral, rapidly became "the symbol of the family separation crisis playing out
on America's southern border". See "Donald Trump makes Time cover
again, this time over US-Mexico border immigration crisis",
http://www.abc.net.au/news/2018-06-22/donald-trump-featured-on-time-
cover-with-immigrant-child/9898534, accessed 22 June 2018. The 2-year-
old was subsequently identified as Yanela Sanchez. It turned out that she
was never actually separated from her mother, Sandra, for which *Time*
magazine published a correction. See Aaron Blake, "Time magazine's major

mistake on the crying-girl cover",
https://www.washingtonpost.com/news/the-fix/wp/2018/06/22/time-magazines-major-screw-up-on-the-crying-girl-cover/?utm_term=.12c97c9d6692, accessed 23 June 2018. See also Ethan Sacks, "Time issues correction for photo of crying 2-year-old migrant. The Honduran girl whose photo has come to symbolize Trump's family separation policy was not separated from her mother, it turns out.", https://www.nbcnews.com/storyline/immigration-border-crisis/time-issues-correction-photo-crying-2-year-old-migrant-n885836, accessed 23 June 2018. Gabriel Moreno Esparza credits the pressure of "dramatically negative coverage" by the media and the power of photographic evidence for Trump's reversal of his separation policy, and points to the capitulation as an indication that Trump and his administration are indeed "susceptible to the mainstream news media they rail against – even to the point of quickly changing actual policy". See Gabriel Moreno Esparza, "How the media dealt a major blow to Trump's family separations policy", https://www.timeslive.co.za/news/world/2018-06-30-how-the-media-dealt-a-major-blow-to-trumps-family-separations-policy/, accessed 30 June 2018.

[67] See Dan Merica, "Trump says both sides to blame amid Charlottesville backlash", https://edition.cnn.com/2017/08/15/politics/trump-charlottesville-delay/index.html, accessed 30 May 2018. On Trump's controversial Zero Tolerance immigration policy, see *The 11th Hour with Brian Williams* June 21, 2018 | MSNBC Today 6/21/2018", https://youtu.be/ifBzGqUJtqs, accessed 22 June 2018.

[68] See David Boddiger, "Trump Breaks Own Off-the-Record Agreement with New York Times Publisher over Meeting [UPDATED]", https://splinternews.com/trump-breaks-own-off-the-record-agreement-with-new-york-1827956226, accessed 30 July 2018.

[69] Such repeated condemnations, accusations, attacks, denials and distractions make perfect sense in terms of Bernays's techniques for propaganda and manipulation, especially if adopted, echoed and reproduced by Trump's echo-chambers on Twitter, Fox News, Sinclair Broadcast Group and Breitbart, and all target his Republican supporters and base. For more on the techniques that inform Trump's communication and media techniques, see "How One Man Manipulated All of America", https://youtu.be/nj_UWbifM2U, accessed 10 June 2018; "Propaganda and Manipulation: How mass media engineers and distorts our perceptions", https://youtu.be/Pfo5gPG72KM, accessed 10 June 2018.

[70] On this point, some see Trump as "a bad version of the Manchurian Candidate", given to acting on impulse without understanding the facts. See *The 11th Hour with Brian Williams 6/28/2018 | MSNBC NEWS* June 28, 2018", https://youtu.be/TIFr6v-aeaY, accessed 29 June 2018.

[71] Despite his determined obsession with presenting himself and being perceived as tough, manly and mature, Trump is repeatedly portrayed by his critics as someone who seeks to dominate attention in a very juvenile way. During President Trump's widely protested maiden working visit to the UK (where is approval rating was only 11%) on 12 July 2018, an anti-Trump campaign group sought and obtained permission for a giant diapered "Trump Baby" balloon – fake Trump filled with real hot air – to fly mockingly over central London. See "Trump Baby Blimp Organizer: Moral Outrage Doesn't Work on Trump | *The Beat with Ari Melber* | MSNBC", https://youtu.be/2NhTC51j10A, accessed 12 July 2018. See also "'Trump Baby' balloon banned from Turnberry", https://www.bbc.co.uk/news/uk-scotland-scotland-politics-44806900, accessed 12 July 2018. See also "Donald Trump in Britain: President Lands as Protests Begin", https://youtu.be/e75S1Br7bF0, accessed 12 July 2018. For a report on an interview in which Trump criticised Theresa May, "President Trump Talks Baby Blimp, Criticizes British PM In New Interview | The Last Word | MSNBC", https://youtu.be/GmXx72e6mKo, accessed 15 July 2018. See also, "Massive Protests in London as President Donald Trump Meets with the Queen, PM | Hardball | MSNBC", https://youtu.be/ydxlfnTHpb4, accessed 15 July 2018.

[72] See Jane C. Timm, "Sarah Palin at Values Voter Summit: Liberals are the intolerant ones!", http://www.msnbc.com/msnbc/palin-liberals-are-the-intolerant-ones, accessed 4 June 2018.

[73] Donald Trump seems to have made easy virtue of the age of social media and the attractive temptations of simplistic narratives. From the incessant sound of fury emanating from American busy newsrooms and late night satirical comedy shows Americans, in their vast majority, think of Trump as someone unleashed, unplugged, and unhinged, and this is especially the case when his fingers begin to fidget with tweets on his smartphone. His Twitterdom (*The Daily Show* et al. 2018) makes him envy nothing from the kings and queens of other realms. In his determination to attack without relent anyone who dares to criticise him, Trump launched a series of attacks against satirical comedians on 25 June 2018 at a rally in South Carolina. Summarily labelling them untalented, the President described Stephen Colbert as a "lowlife", Jimmy Fallon as a "lost soul" and Jimmy Kimmel night show, as "terrible". In response to the criticism, comedians put up a united front to respond to the President's attacks. See "Jimmy Fallon, Stephen Colbert and Conan O'Brien unite against Donald Trump", https://www-bbc-com.cdn.ampproject.org/v/s/www.bbc.com/news/amp/entertainment-arts-44626779?amp_js_v=0.1#amp_tf=From%20%251%24s&ampshare=https%3A%2F%2Fwww.bbc.com%2Fnews%2Fentertainment-arts-44626779, accessed 27 June 2018; see also "'Lowlife' Colbert Video Chats With 'Lost

Soul' Fallon & Conan O'Brien", https://youtu.be/YxoEXO-htKg, accessed 27 June 2018. Like Dracula with every droplet of blood, he is said to rise to the virility and sense of purpose activated by reactions to his daily avalanche of tweet storms. The mainstream liberal media in particular have described him as a hateful, vile and racist person with a very loose relationship with the truth, someone who struggles to distinguish fact from fiction, and whose spectacularly incurious mind in no way helps matters. He is represented as someone who would rather fabricate what his surrogates have labelled "alternative facts" than live with the reality of what he and his supporters systematically dismiss as "fake news", a term he purports to have originated (Spicer 2018). In his first year as president, Trump reportedly stated 2,000 falsehoods, when some of his predecessors could barely count 100 in two four-year terms. According to *The Washington Post*, President Trump made an average of more than 6.5 false or misleading claims a day, and a total of "3,251 false or misleading claims in 497 days" (see Glenn Kessler, Salvador Rizzo and Meg Kelly, "President Trump has made 3,251 false or misleading claims in 497 days", https://www.washingtonpost.com/news/fact-checker/wp/2018/06/01/president-trump-has-made-3251-false-or-misleading-claims-in-497-days/?utm_term=.b588d799158d, accessed 26 July 2018). In July 2018 Steven Rattner presented on MSBNC's *Morning Joe* statistics compiled by the *Toronto Star*, indicating that President Trump is lying more and more often. Accordingly, "The Star analyzed the 1,340,330 words that Mr. Trump has spoken (and tweeted) since he took office and found 1,929 false statements involving 68,928 words" (see Steven Rattner, "*Morning Joe* Charts: Trump's Prolific Rise in Falsehoods", https://stevenrattner.com/2018/07/morning-joe-charts-trumps-prolific-rise-in-falsehoods/, accessed 19 July 2018). For a sense of the place of comedy as a form of entertainment and news in the USA, see Amarnath Amarasingam (2011).See "100 days of Trump claims", https://www.washingtonpost.com/graphics/politics/trump-claims/?noredirect=on&utm_term=.93ea6789cd89, accessed 29 May 2018.
[74] It is striking to see just how much of Trump's communication strategies and techniques are similar to Bernays's techniques for propaganda and manipulation. For more on the techniques that inform Trump's communication and media techniques, see "How One Man Manipulated All of America", https://youtu.be/nj_UWbifM2U, accessed 10 June 2018; "Propaganda and Manipulation: How mass media engineers and distorts our perceptions", https://youtu.be/Pfo5gPG72KM, accessed 10 June 2018.
[75] A poll published on 26 June 2018 indicated that 8 in 10 Americans were "very" or "somewhat" concerned about conditions of American democracy, with 50% of Americans believing that the USA was in "real danger of becoming a nondemocratic, authoritarian country" in the age of President

Trump. See "Americans' Faith in Democracy Erodes in the Age of President Donald Trump | Deadline | MSNBC", https://youtu.be/nmUVYFBVD5Q, accessed 27 June 2018.

[76] See "Consumerism", https://www.youtube.com/watch?v=8l5fRI-YnG0&feature=youtu.be, accessed 27 May 2018.

[77] According to Michael Avenatti, lawyer for Stormy Daniel, a pornstar with whom Donald Trump allegedly paid off for an alleged an affair, "Trump demands loyalty from everyone and provides loyalty to no one except Vladimir Putin", see "Avenatti Reveals Another Client's Case Involves Donald Trump, AMI | *The Beat with Ari Melber* | MSNBC", https://youtu.be/s1TefD8LbQU, accessed 28 July 2018.

[78] The liberal American media overwhelmingly represent Trump as someone who belongs more in the company of autocrats, totalitarians, kings, princes and dictators, than with the autonomy-seeking millennial liberals whose sensitivities to the sensibilities of freedom and choice are alert to and critical of any form of authority, not to mention authoritarianism. He reportedly, loves having his name in giant gold letters on towers all over the world– Trump Tower, Trump Tower Dreams – and seems particularly keen to see his name in glowing letters on a Moscow Trump Tower, a dream he pursued for decades. As president, he is said to tend towards keeping the company of and excelling among those who believe that government should control the message and the messenger in the sole interest of the whims and caprice of the BIG MAN at the centre of power and privilege, playing God in the lives of all and sundry. His singular obsession is an expectation of everyone to be scrupulously and blindly loyal to his craving for power without responsibility. "I need loyalty, I expect loyalty", says James Comey, former Director of the FBI, mimicking his boss after being fired for not guaranteeing that loyalty (Comey 2018). In the heart and heat of the Russian meddling investigation, Trump reportedly asserted his absolute right to pardon anyone, including himself. On this, one of his tweets on 4 June 2018 read:

> As has been stated by numerous legal scholars, I have the absolute right to PARDON myself, but why would I do that when I have done nothing wrong? In the meantime, the never ending Witch Hunt, led by 13 very Angry and Conflicted Democrats (& others) continues into the mid-terms!
> (See Hannah Levintova, "Trump Asserts 'Absolute' Right to Pardon Himself in Russia Probe", https://www.motherjones.com/politics/2018/06/trump-asserts-absolute-right-to-pardon-himself-in-russia-probe/, accessed 6 June 2018).

Following his summit with Kim Jong Un in Singapore on 12 June 2018, Trump expressed envy for the authoritativeness and respect enjoyed by the

North Korean dictator from his people, wishing he could have some of it from his fellow Americans. Speaking to Steve Doocy of "Fox & Friends" outside the White House, Trump said of Kim, "He speaks and his people sit up at attention. I want my people to do the same". See Max Greenwood, "Trump: Kim's people sit up when he speaks, 'I want my people to do the same'", https://thehill-com.cdn.ampproject.org/v/thehill.com/homenews/administration/392430-trump-i-want-americans-to-listen-to-me-like-north-koreans-listen-to?amp=&amp_js_v=0.1#amp_tf=From%20%251%24s&ampshare=http%3A%2F%2Fthehill.com%2Fhomenews%2Fadministration%2F392430-trump-i-want-americans-to-listen-to-me-like-north-koreans-listen-to, accessed 15 June 2018.

[79] See Thomas L. Friedman, "Whatever Trump Is Hiding Is Hurting All of Us Now", https://www.nytimes.com/2018/02/18/opinion/trump-russia-putin.html, accessed 29 May 2018.

[80] See Lili Loofbourow, "The America We Thought We Knew Is Gone", https://slate.com/news-and-politics/2018/06/supreme-court-is-now-trumps-and-so-we-grieve-for-america.html, accessed 30 June 2018.

[81] See *The Century of the Self*, Part 2: "The Engineering of Consent", https://www.youtube.com/watch?v=fEsPOt8MG7E, accessed 14 April 2018.

[82] See "Programming the nation 2011 HD", https://www.youtube.com/watch?v=bygwXLyWTSQ, accessed 7 May 2018.

[83] See Robinson Meyer, "The Grim Conclusions of the Largest-Ever Study of Fake News", https://www.theatlantic.com/technology/archive/2018/03/largest-study-ever-fake-news-mit-twitter/555104/?utm_source=atlfb, accessed 13 April 2018.

[84] See David Robson, "The Myth of the Online Echo Chamber", http://www.bbc.com/future/story/20180416-the-myth-of-the-online-echo-chamber, accessed 18 April 2018.

[85] For a sense of how many Russians allegedly involved in the elaborate scheme by Putin to influence the outcome of the election also happened to have attended Trump's inauguration, and some as VIPs to some events, see "The Chairman's Global Dinner" in "*The Rachel Maddow Show* 6/28/2018 | MSNBC NEWS June 28, 2018", https://youtu.be/vhY_6ktbef0, accessed 29 June 2018. On the weekend before a Monday 16 July 2018 Trump–Putin summit in Helsinki, Robert Mueller, the special counsel tasked with investigating Russian meddling with the 2016 election, issued a 29-page detailed indictment against 12 Russians working for the Russian Military Intelligence Service (GRU), charging them with undertaking "large-scale cyber operations", that included the hacking and stealing of documents

from the Democratic National Committee (DNC) servers on the Hilary Clinton campaign (for more on the hacking, see Brazile 2017; Clinton 2017; Sanger 2018), designed "to interfere with the 2016 US presidential election". Not even such an indictment was enough for Trump to call off the Helsinki summit, or to discontinue his repetitive lullaby-like refrain of "no collusion", "rigged witch hunt" and "hoax" (see CNN, "Tony Schwartz: 'No collusion' is Trump's lullaby", https://youtu.be/vGkU09xDBEQ, accessed 15 July 2018). Not only did he go ahead with his Helsinki meeting, he readily reiterated and endorsed Putin's "extremely strong and powerful denial" of meddling and dismissal of the Mueller indictment of 12 Russian intelligence officers as "utter nonsense", repeating instead his criticism of his own law enforcement and intelligence institutions and blaming them for the bad state of relations between the USA and Russia in a manner that baffled the overwhelming majority of the mainstream media, politicians, diplomats and concerned people on social media in America, its European allies and globally (see "Trump Avoids Rebuking Putin on Election Interference: Live Updates", https://www.nytimes.com/2018/07/16/world/europe/trump-putin-summit-helsinki.html, accessed 16 July 2018; see also, Aaron Blake, "President Trump's news conference with Russia's Putin, annotated", https://www.washingtonpost.com/news/the-fix/wp/2018/07/16/full-text-president-trumps-news-conference-with-russias-putin/?utm_term=.9cddab9f18fb, accessed 16 July 2018; see also Emily Birnbaum and Brett Samuels, "CNN, NBC, Fox personalities slam Trump over performance at Putin press conference", https://thehill-com.cdn.ampproject.org/v/thehill.com/homenews/media/397220-media-slams-trump-over-performance-at-putin-press-conference?amp=&amp_js_v=0.1#amp_tf=From%20%251%24s&ampshare=http%3A%2F%2Fthehill.com%2Fhomenews%2Fmedia%2F397220-media-slams-trump-over-performance-at-putin-press-conference, accessed 16 July 2018; see also *The Rachel Maddow Show* July 16, 2018 MSNBC Rachel Maddow MSNBC 7/16/2018", https://youtu.be/_Yj68A2PKjs, accessed 17 July 2018). Trump's personalisation of the investigation into the election meddling has often obstructed his ability to judge and accept what actually happened in his capacity as President and leader of the USA, even if detrimental to his private and personal feelings and desires. He has repeatedly chosen self-preservation and what is best for him than to do what is right for the USA and its national interests. Trump's stubborn insistence on self-preservation and reluctance to cave even to an avalanche of bipartisan fury has drawn criticism from many, including George Will, who has described Trump as a "sad, embarrassing wreck of a man", and as "America's child president" who does not hesitate to "put himself first, as always, and America last," especially in relation to Russia's meddling with

the 2016 election. According to Will, his rhetoric of "America first",
notwithstanding, Trump did not hesitate to put America "behind President
Vladimir Putin's regime," and to readily cast doubt on his own intelligence
agency and handpicked director of National Intelligence, Dan Coats (see
https://www.washingtonpost.com/opinions/this-sad-embarrassing-wreck-
of-a-man/2018/07/17/d06de8ea-89e8-11e8-a345-
a1bf7847b375_story.html?utm_term=.e35b4c4ae769, accessed 19 July 2018;
see also *"The Beat with Ari Melber* July 18 2018",
https://youtu.be/65faMcg5GWg, accessed 19 July 2018; "George Will
Considers The 'Embarrassing Wreck Of A Man'" *Morning Joe*, MSNBC,
https://youtu.be/GsgccOuZ0qg, accessed 19 July 2018). For more on the
indictment, see CNN, "Mueller indicts 12 Russian military officers for DNC
hacking", https://youtu.be/mYXCsxf9TsE, accessed 15 July 2018; see also,
Rosalind S. Helderman and Manuel Roig-Franzia, "Charges against Russian
intelligence officers intensify spotlight on Trump adviser Roger Stone",
https://www.washingtonpost.com/politics/charges-against-russian-
intelligence-officers-intensify-spotlight-on-trump-adviser-roger-
stone/2018/07/13/ba0d0caa-86bb-11e8-8553-
a3ce89036c78_story.html?noredirect=on&utm_term=.2436bc5c5cee,
accessed 15 July 2018. Indeed, not even a bombshell revelation by "Michael
Cohen, President Donald Trump's former personal attorney, … that then-
candidate Trump knew in advance about the June 2016 meeting in Trump
Tower in which Russians were expected to offer his campaign dirt on
Hillary Clinton", and that he, Cohen, "is willing to make that assertion to
special counsel Robert Mueller", seemed enough for Trump to discontinue
his denials of collusion and claims of witch hunts (see Jim Scuitto, Carl
Bernstein and Marshall Cohen, "The Russian Investigation: Cohen claims
Trump knew in advance of 2016 Trump Tower meeting,"
https://edition.cnn.com/2018/07/26/politics/michael-cohen-donald-
trump-june-2016-meeting-knowledge/index.html, accessed 27 July 2018).
[86] See David Corn, "Donald Trump Is Getting Away with the Biggest
Scandal in American History",
https://www.motherjones.com/politics/2018/06/trump-russia-scandal-
media/, accessed 6 June 2018.
[87] Both Trump and Putin have repeatedly insisted that there was neither
meddling nor collusion. Only under exceptional public pressure has Trump
reluctantly admitted that Russia did meddle. Even then, his rare admissions
are quickly followed by "it could have been anyone, there are lots of people
out there", along with, "there was no collusion", "it's all a hoax", and "total
witch hunt". It is hardly surprising therefore, that, according to NBC News,
"19 months into his presidency, there is no coherent Trump administration
strategy to combat foreign election interference — and no single person or
agency in charge". See Ken Dilanian, "Trump admin has no central strategy

116

for election security, and no one's in charge: After two years of calling Russian election meddling a hoax, President Trump will preside over a meeting about election security",
https://www.nbcnews.com/politics/elections/trump-admin-has-no-central-strategy-election-security-no-one-n895256, accessed 28 July 2018. See also *The Last Word with Lawrence O'Donnell* 7/27/18 [Full] MSNBC NEWS W/Lawrence O'Donnell July 27, 2018,
https://youtu.be/CtrG1kXmEAk, accessed 28 July 2018; and *The Rachel Maddow Show* July 27, 2018 [FULL] Rachel Maddow MSNBC NEWS 7/27/18, https://youtu.be/lyGg4gbzGIU, accessed 28 July 2018.

[88] See Uri Friedman, "Russian Speakers Explain What Putin Actually Said about Trump: In Helsinki, the Russian president didn't confess to meddling. But he left no doubt about who he wanted to win the U.S. election",
https://www.theatlantic.com/international/archive/2018/07/putin-trump-election-translation/565481/, accessed 25 July 2018.

[89] See *"The Rachel Maddow Show*, MSNBC 7/24/18 Breaking news Trump & Cohen Talking Model Payoff", https://youtu.be/20azCKrw6Rk, accessed 25 July 2018.

[90] See *The Century of the Self*, Part 2: "The Engineering of Consent", https://www.youtube.com/watch?v=fEsPOt8MG7E, accessed 14 April 2018.

[91] See Ronald Blumer, "The Invention of Public Relations", https://www.youtube.com/watch?v=iBEclayBCdc&feature=youtu.be, accessed 16 April 2018.

[92] See *The Century of the Self*, Part 2: "The Engineering of Consent", https://www.youtube.com/watch?v=fEsPOt8MG7E, accessed 14 April 2018.

[93] See *The Century of the Self*, Part 2: "The Engineering of Consent", https://www.youtube.com/watch?v=fEsPOt8MG7E, accessed 14 April 2018.

[94] In this regard and in view of the persuasion in political psychology that the role of personality psychology is crucial in understanding the continuing evolution of democracy (Caprara and Vecchione 2017), it is noteworthy that 27 psychiatrists and psychologists came together in 2017 and offered their consensus view that President Trump's mental state posed a clear and urgent danger to the wellbeing of Americans and the American state, and that this disqualified him to be an effective president. The title of their book speaks for itself: *The Dangerous Case of Donald Trump: 27 Psychiatrists and Mental Health Experts Assess a President* (Lee et al. 2017). When a person who is apparently at the apex of the ruling elite turns out, surprisingly, to be emotionally dis-regulated, or opts not to play according to the established rules of the game of the rationality of power, preferring instead to rely on the whims and caprices of his impulses, psychologists whose whole intellectual project and practice are predicated upon cultivating and

117

maintaining the establishment, do not hesitate to question the psychological competence of such a purported member of the establishment. This was their case against Trump (see also Dionne Jr et al. 2017).

[95] See *The Century of the Self*, Part 2: "The Engineering of Consent", https://www.youtube.com/watch?v=fEsPOt8MG7E, accessed 14 April 2018.

[96] See *The Century of the Self*, Part 2: "The Engineering of Consent", https://www.youtube.com/watch?v=fEsPOt8MG7E, accessed 14 April 2018.

[97] See *The Century of the Self*, Part 2: "The Engineering of Consent", https://www.youtube.com/watch?v=fEsPOt8MG7E, accessed 14 April 2018.

[98] See *The Century of the Self*, Part 2: "The Engineering of Consent", https://www.youtube.com/watch?v=fEsPOt8MG7E, accessed 14 April 2018.

[99] See *The Century of the Self*, Part 2: "The Engineering of Consent", https://www.youtube.com/watch?v=fEsPOt8MG7E, accessed 14 April 2018.

[100] See *The Century of the Self*, Part 3: "There is a Policeman inside All Our Heads; He Must Be Destroyed", https://www.youtube.com/watch?v=ub2LB2MaGoM, accessed 14 April 2018.

[101] See *The Century of the Self*, Part 2: "The Engineering of Consent", https://www.youtube.com/watch?v=fEsPOt8MG7E, accessed 14 April 2018. See also, "Consumerism", https://www.youtube.com/watch?v=8l5fRI-YnG0&feature=youtu.be, accessed 27 May 2018.

[102] See *The Century of the Self*, Part 2: "The Engineering of Consent", https://www.youtube.com/watch?v=fEsPOt8MG7E, accessed 14 April 2018.

[103] See *The Century of the Self*, Part 3: "There is a Policeman inside All Our Heads; He Must Be Destroyed", https://www.youtube.com/watch?v=ub2LB2MaGoM, accessed 14 April 2018.

[104] See *The Century of the Self*, Part 3: "There is a Policeman inside All Our Heads; He Must Be Destroyed", https://www.youtube.com/watch?v=ub2LB2MaGoM, accessed 14 April 2018.

[105] See *The Century of the Self*, Part 2: "The Engineering of Consent", https://www.youtube.com/watch?v=fEsPOt8MG7E, accessed 14 April 2018; see also "Martin Luther King, Jr. on Creative Maladjustment", a speech delivered on 18 December 1963, at Western Michigan University,

http://thepossibilitypractice.com/martin-luther-king-jr-on-creative-maladjustment/, accessed 1 April 2018.

[106] See *The Century of the Self*, Part 2: "The Engineering of Consent", https://www.youtube.com/watch?v=fEsPOt8MG7E, accessed 14 April 2018.

[107] Widely available online. See, for example, https://www.pressreader.com/south-africa/volksblad/20161007/281638189709999, accessed 4 June 2018.

[108] See Eli Watkins and Abby Phillip, "Trump decries immigrants from 'shithole countries' coming to US", https://edition.cnn.com/2018/01/11/politics/immigrants-shithole-countries-trump/index.html, accessed 14 April 2018.

[109] See *The Century of the Self*, Part 3: "There is a Policeman inside All Our Heads; He Must Be Destroyed", https://www.youtube.com/watch?v=ub2LB2MaGoM, accessed 14 April 2018.

[110] It is worth stating, however, that finding out what people think is not necessarily incompatible with using that knowledge to manipulate them for propaganda, ideological and commercial ends.

[111] See Gary H. Grossman, Rob Blumenstein and Sean P Geary, "Sell & Spin: A History of Advertising", https://www.youtube.com/watch?v=YPBf7km7NAk&t=890s, accessed 12 May 2018.

[112] See *The Century of the Self*, Part 3: "There is a Policeman inside All Our Heads; He Must Be Destroyed", https://www.youtube.com/watch?v=ub2LB2MaGoM, accessed 14 April 2018.

[113] See *The Century of the Self*, Part 3: "There is a Policeman inside All Our Heads; He Must Be Destroyed", https://www.youtube.com/watch?v=ub2LB2MaGoM, accessed 14 April 2018.

[114] See *The Century of the Self*, Part 3: "There is a Policeman inside All Our Heads; He Must Be Destroyed", https://www.youtube.com/watch?v=ub2LB2MaGoM, accessed 14 April 2018.

[115] See *The Century of the Self*, Part 3: "There is a Policeman inside All Our Heads; He Must Be Destroyed", https://www.youtube.com/watch?v=ub2LB2MaGoM, accessed 14 April 2018.

[116] See *The Century of the Self*, Part 2: "The Engineering of Consent", https://www.youtube.com/watch?v=fEsPOt8MG7E, accessed 14 April 2018; see also *The Century of the Self*. Part 4: "Eight People Sipping Wine in

Kettering", https://www.youtube.com/watch?v=VouaAz5mQAs, accessed 13 March 2018.

[117] See *The Century of the Self*, Part 3: "There is a Policeman inside All Our Heads; He Must Be Destroyed", https://www.youtube.com/watch?v=ub2LB2MaGoM, accessed 14 April 2018.

[118] See *The Century of the Self*, Part 3: "There is a Policeman inside All Our Heads; He Must Be Destroyed", https://www.youtube.com/watch?v=ub2LB2MaGoM, accessed 14 April 2018.

[119] See *The Century of the Self*, Part 3: "There is a Policeman inside All Our Heads; He Must Be Destroyed", https://www.youtube.com/watch?v=ub2LB2MaGoM, accessed 14 April 2018.

[120] See *The Century of the Self*, Part 3: "There is a Policeman inside All Our Heads; He Must Be Destroyed", https://www.youtube.com/watch?v=ub2LB2MaGoM, accessed 14 April 2018; See also *The Century of the Self*, Part 4: "Eight People Sipping Wine in Kettering", https://www.youtube.com/watch?v=VouaAz5mQAs, accessed 13 March 2018.

[121] See Reagan's 8 June 1982 speech on his new individualism and the need for a global infrastructure for democracy globally, "Address to Members of the British Parliament June 8, 1982", https://www.reaganlibrary.gov/sites/default/files/archives/speeches/1982/60882a.htm, accessed 9 June 2018.

[122] See "The Saatchi & Saatchi Story", https://www.youtube.com/watch?v=sB8rWFEnuqI, accessed 2 June 2018; "Lord Saatchi discusses Lady Thatcher on *BBC Hardtalk*", https://www.youtube.com/watch?v=_I-nUiaazLk, accessed 2 June 2018; "Lord Saatchi on 'selling' Margaret Thatcher", https://www.youtube.com/watch?v=kiipURBHZdY, accessed 2 June 2018.

[123] See *The Century of the Self*, Part 3: "There is a Policeman inside All Our Heads; He Must Be Destroyed", https://www.youtube.com/watch?v=ub2LB2MaGoM, accessed 14 April 2018; See also *The Century of the Self*, Part 4: "Eight People Sipping Wine in Kettering", https://www.youtube.com/watch?v=VouaAz5mQAs, accessed 13 March 2018.

[124] See *The Century of the Self*, Part 3: "There is a Policeman inside All Our Heads; He Must Be Destroyed", https://www.youtube.com/watch?v=ub2LB2MaGoM, accessed 14 April 2018.

[125] See *The Century of the Self*, Part 4: "Eight People Sipping Wine in Kettering", https://www.youtube.com/watch?v=VouaAz5mQAs, accessed 13 March 2018.

[126] See "Tony Blair on Brexit, Labour, and populism – *BBC Newsnight*", https://youtu.be/63TBWCnlPO8, 22 July 2018.

[127] See *The Century of the Self*, Part 3: "There is a Policeman inside All Our Heads; He Must Be Destroyed", https://www.youtube.com/watch?v=ub2LB2MaGoM, accessed 14 April 2018.

[128] See *The Century of the Self*, Part 4: "Eight People Sipping Wine in Kettering", https://www.youtube.com/watch?v=VouaAz5mQAs, accessed 13 March 2018.

[129] See *The Century of the Self*, Part 4: "Eight People Sipping Wine in Kettering", https://www.youtube.com/watch?v=VouaAz5mQAs, accessed 13 March 2018.

[130] See *The Century of the Self*, Part 4: "Eight People Sipping Wine in Kettering", https://www.youtube.com/watch?v=VouaAz5mQAs, accessed 13 March 2018.

[131] In July 2018, UK born Hungarian American citizen, former Trump adviser Sebastian Gorka, described Donald Trump as "the master communicator" with "53 million followers on Twitter", and as "a man who has never squirmed in his life" (See Channel 4 News, "Former Trump adviser Sebastian Gorka lauds the President's UK visit", https://youtu.be/8AjsGxmxBOk, accessed 15 July 2018). Trump may not be the Hollywood actor that Reagan was, but he has perfected the art of acting as a self-promotion public relations gimmick by manipulating the media to serve his ends and to build a public image of himself as the world's greatest ever dealmaker (Trump with Schwartz 1987; Johnston 2016). This has earned him the reputation of "the wizard of hype" whose carefully engineered world of "glitz and glamour" hides from the fascinated public many telling contradictions to his public persona (O'Brien 2016[2007]). His obsession with spin and ruthless pursuit of money and power as the currency of his life strike some of his critics as indicative of someone who is more interested in the show and in showmanship than in actual achievements, convictions, strategy, decisiveness and consistency in thought and practice.

[132] See "Donald Trump REALLY POWERFUL Full Documentary 2016", ttps://youtu.be/Ng3LjuUgxwc, accessed 11 June 2018. Indeed, as happened at his Helsinki meeting with Russia where he capitulated by siding with Putin against the Mueller indictment of 12 Russian intelligence officers and in dismissing accusations of collusion, he does not hesitate to take the side of Putin and Russia against the very USA whose interests are supposedly his responsibilities as president to defend. See for example, "*The*

Rachel Maddow Show July 16, 2018 MSNBC Rachel Maddow MSNBC 7/16/2018", https://youtu.be/_Yj68A2PKjs, accessed 17 July 2018.

[133] See "Jesus saith unto him, I am the way, the truth, and the life: no man cometh unto the Father, but by me", *Bible*, John 14:6 King James Version (KJV).

[134] See "Consumerism", https://www.youtube.com/watch?v=815fRI-YnG0&feature=youtu.be, accessed 27 May 2018; see also Gene Brockhoff, "Impact of Consumerism", https://www.youtube.com/watch?v=0PgQPsYzyfg&feature=youtu.be, accessed 28 May 2018.

[135] He is known to love winning and to love being liked, and his words repeatedly make no secret of that. As Esme Cribb reports, in a speech to American troops at the U.S. Central Command and Special Operations Command headquarters at MacDill Air Force Base, Florida, Trump said: "We had a wonderful election, didn't we?" "I saw those numbers, and you like me, and I like you. That's the way it works." See Esme Cribb, "Trump Promises Gear, Praises Self, and Rips the Media in Speech at Centcom", https://talkingpointsmemo.com/livewire/trump-promises-equipment-praises-self-rips-media-in-centcom-speech, accessed 27 July 2018.

[136] Trump might have a point about the hidden powers of the *Deep State*, if depictions of the inner workings of state institutions are to be taken seriously. That power even in established democracies is not always formal, obvious or predictable is eloquently dramatised in the BBC TV satirical series, *Yes, Prime Minister* (Lynn & Jay 1989), in which civil servants make sure that ideas of the Prime Minister and his Ministers (elected politicians) never come to fruition, unless there is something in those ideas that is of interest and benefit to the civil servants themselves, who, though unelected, can make or mar. Such career civil servants or bureaucrats are veritable hidden persuaders, as they tend to credit neither the elected politicians nor their electors ("the masses" or "the people") with the knowledge, rationality and sophistication to make the right choices and decisions. They are the unelected government purportedly at the (dis)service of elected politicians and the electorate. For snippet view of how cynical such civil servants are towards politicians, the electorate and democracy, see "How the Media and Literati Class Determines the Politics of a Nation", https://youtu.be/TwFDvMiBKeM, accessed 18 June 2018. That said, it could, in the case of Trump's persistent rejection and only reluctant acceptance of Russian meddling in the 2016 election to favour him, be argued that it is the higher patriotic duty of the functionaries of the *deep state*, to speak up and speak out about what actually happened, even if a complicit president accuses them of politicking and of monetisation of their positions, and even if that president threatens to revoke their access to intelligence. This is what happened on July 23, 2018, when "President

Trump threatened … to strip the security clearances of top former officials who criticized his refusal to confront Russia over its election interference, signaling a willingness to use the powers of the presidency to retaliate against some of his most outspoken detractors". Among them were John O. Brennan, the former C.I.A. director; Susan E. Rice, the former national security adviser; and James R. Clapper Jr., the former director of national intelligence. See Julie Hirschfeld Davis and Julian E. Barnes, "Trump Weighs Stripping Security Clearances from Officials Who Criticized Him", https://www.nytimes.com/2018/07/23/us/politics/trump-security-clearances.html, accessed 25 July 2018; see also Steve Schmidt, "Dangerous Day For American Democracy" *Deadline* MSNBC, https://youtu.be/mqLInDwRoUw, accessed 25 July 2018.

[137] See Thomas L. Friedman, "Whatever Trump Is Hiding Is Hurting All of Us Now", https://www.nytimes.com/2018/02/18/opinion/trump-russia-putin.html, accessed 29 May 2018. See also *"The Rachel Maddow Show* July 16, 2018 MSNBC Rachel Maddow MSNBC 7/16/2018", https://youtu.be/_Yj68A2PKjs, accessed 17 July 2018. See also *"All In with Chris Hayes* MSNBC July 16, 2018 MSNBC News *All In with Chris Hayes* 7-16-2018", https://youtu.be/OP1vGhP-uqM, accessed 17 July 2018. Unlike Ronald Reagan, his purported Republican role model who considered Russia as the focus of evil in the modern world, Trump, for whatever reason, has consistently not hesitated to side with Putin, even if it means doing so to the detriment of his own country's interests, security and age-old law and order and intelligence institutions.

[138] See David Frum, "How Donald Trump turned the United States into a headless giant", https://www.Theglobeandmail.Com/Opinion/David-Frum-How-Donald-Trump-Turned-The-United-States-Into-A-Headless-Giant/Article37588493/, accessed 13 January 2018.

[139] See David E. Sanger and Matthew Rosenberg, "From the Start, Trump Has Muddied a Clear Message: Putin Interfered", https://www.nytimes.com/2018/07/18/world/europe/trump-intelligence-russian-election-meddling-.html, accessed 20 July 2018.

[140] See Will Hurd, "Trump Is Being Manipulated by Putin. What Should We Do?" https://www.nytimes.com/2018/07/19/opinion/trump-russia-putin-republican-congress.html, accessed 20 July 2018.

[141] See Matthew Yglesias, "Confessions of a Russiagate true believer. Trump isn't an idiot — the cover-up is likely covering up serious wrongdoing", https://www.vox.com/policy-and-politics/2018/2/21/17030420/trump-russia-mueller-guilty, accessed 22 February 2018.

[142] This is so blatant that it has been picked upon as a regular topic of satirical comedy by many a late night American cable television comedy show. Comedian Trevor Noah, South African born host of *The Daily Show*, for example, has commented repeatedly on how very strikingly Trump is

like an African President. See "Donald Trump – America's African President: The Daily Show", https://youtu.be/2FPrJxTvgdQ, accessed 17 June 2018. For a study of the systematic control of the media and the proliferation of propaganda cementing the personalisation of power by presidents who pay lip service to democracy, see Nyamnjoh (2005). For more on the Africanness of Trump-style leadership and related matters, see *The Late with Stephen Colbert*, "Trevor Noah Was Low-key In 'Black Panther'", https://youtu.be/wC6V4gLAat4, accessed 22 June 2018.

143 For a sense in the US media and commentators that Trump is actively colluding with Putin not only to dismantle America's democratic institutions and infrastructure but also international organisations and relations with America's allies, see *The 11th Hour with Brian Williams* 6/28/2018 | MSNBC NEWS June 28, 2018, https://youtu.be/TIFr6v-aeaY, accessed 29 June 2018. See also David Ignatius, "Trump is scarred, prickly and needy", https://www.washingtonpost.com/opinions/trumps-neediness-is-at-the-core-of-his-diplomacy/2018/07/10/b153f844-8477-11e8-8553-a3ce89036c78_story.html?noredirect=on&utm_term=.e005ce921458, accessed 12 July 2018.

144 See Robinson Meyer "Mark Zuckerberg Says He's Not Resigning", https://www.theatlantic.com/technology/archive/2018/04/mark-zuckerberg-atlantic-exclusive/557489/, accessed 9 April 2018.

145 See "Consumerism", https://www.youtube.com/watch?v=8l5fRI-YnG0&feature=youtu.be, accessed 27 May 2018.

146 See also "Edward Bernays: the Father of Spin – Larry Tye Book Interview (1998)", https://www.youtube.com/watch?v=lQgMxKQ7mX8, accessed 9 June 2018.

147 "Subconscious Fascism - Edward Bernays", https://www.youtube.com/watch?v=ZZNHhzOj3o0, accessed 17 April 2018.

148 See "Stories that sparked #MeToo movement win Pulitzer Prize", https://www.timeslive.co.za/news/world/2018-04-17-stories-that-sparked-metoo-movement-win-pulitzer-prize/, accessed 18 April 2018.

149 See also "Edward Bernays: the Father of Spin – Larry Tye Book Interview (1998)", https://www.youtube.com/watch?v=lQgMxKQ7mX8, accessed 9 June 2018; see also "Mark Crispin Miller & Anne Bernays, Edward Bernays' *Propaganda*", https://www.youtube.com/watch?v=4ZBDDUNdXyU, accessed 9 June 2018.

150 See also "Mark Crispin Miller & Anne Bernays, Edward Bernays' *Propaganda*", https://www.youtube.com/watch?v=4ZBDDUNdXyU, accessed 9 June 2018.

References

Albright, M. (2018) *Fascism: A Warning*, New York: Harper.

Amarasingam, A. (ed) (2011) *The Stewart/Colbert Effect: Essays on the Real Impacts of Fake News*, Jefferson, North Carolina: McFarland & Company, Inc., Publishers.

Barsamian, D. (1994a) *The Prosperous Few and the Restless Many: Noam Chomsky Interviewed by David Barsamian*, Tucson, Arizona: Odonian Press.

Barsamian, D. (1994b) *Secrets, Lies and Democracy: Noam Chomsky Interviewed by David Barsamian*, Tucson, Arizona: Odonian Press.

Beloff, M. (1954) *The Age of Absolutism: 1660–1815*, London: Hutchinson & Co.

Berlin, I. (2002) *Freedom and Its Betrayal: Six Enemies of Human Liberty*. London: Chlano & Windus.

Bernays, E.L. (1961[1923]) *Crystallizing Public Opinion*, New York: Liveright Publishing.

Bernays, E.L. (2004[1928]) *Propaganda*, New York: Ig Publishing.

Bernays, E.L. (1947) "The Engineering of Consent", *The ANNALS of the American Academy of Political and Social Science*, Vol 250(1): 113–120.

Bernays, E.L. (1952) *Public Relations*, Oklahoma: University of Oklahoma Press.

Brazile, D. (2017) *Hacks: The Inside Story of the Break-ins and Breakdowns That Put Donald Trump in the White House*, New York: Hachette Books.

Brock, D. (2005) *The Republican Noise Machine: Right-Wing Media and How It Corrupts Democracy*, New York: Three Rivers Press.

Browder, B. (2015) *Red Notice: A True Story of High Finance, Murder, and One Man's Fight for Justice*, New York: Simon & Schuster.

Bruder, J. (2017) *Nomadland: Surviving America in the Twenty-First Century*, New York: W.W. Norton & Company.

Caprara, G.V. and Vecchione, M. (2017) *Personalizing Politics and Realizing Democracy*, Oxford: Oxford University Press.

Carpenter, A. (2018) *Gaslighting America: Why We Love It When Trump Lies to Us*, New York: Broadside Books.

Chomsky, N. (1989) *Necessary Illusions Thought Control in Democratic Societies*, Cambridge, Massachusetts: South End Press.

Chomsky, N. (1999) *Profit over People: Neoliberalism and Global Order*, New York: Seven Stories Press.

Chomsky, N. (2002) *Media Control: The Spectacular Achievements of Propaganda*, New York: Seven Stories Press.

Chomsky, N. (2004) *Hegemony or Survival: America's Quest for Global Dominance*, New York: Henry Holt and Company.

Clapper, J.R. with Brown, T. (2018) *Facts and Fears: Hard Truths from a Life in Intelligence*, New York: Viking.

Claydon, T. and Levillain, C.-É. (eds) (2015) *Louis XIV Outside In: Images of the Sun King Beyond France, 1661-1715*, Surrey: Ashgate.

Clinton, B. and Patterson, J. (2018) *The President Is Missing: A Novel*, New York: Little, Brown and Company and Knopf.

Clinton, H.R. (2017) *What Happened*, New York: Simon & Schuster.

Comey, J. (2018) *A Higher Loyalty: Truth, Lies and Leadership*, London: MacMillan.

Corsi, J.R. (2018) *Killing the Deep State: The Fight to Save President Trump*, West Palm Beach, Florida: Humanix Books.

Debord, G. (1990) *Comments on the Society of the Spectacle*, New York: Verso.

Denton, R.E. Jr. (1988) *The Prime Time Presidency of Ronald Reagan: The Era of the Television Presidency*, New York: Praeger Publishers.

Descartes, R. (2003[1637]) *Discourse on Method and Meditations*, New York: Dover Publications.

Dionne Jr., E.J., Ornstein, N.J. and Mann, T.E (2017) *One Nation After Trump: A Guide for the Perplexed, the Disillusioned, the Desperate, and the Not-Yet Deported*, New York: St. Martin's Press.

Dyson, M.E. (2018) *What Truth Sounds Like: Robert F. Kennedy, James Baldwin, and Our Unfinished Conversation about Race in America*, New York: St. Martin's Press.

Featherstone, M. (2007) *Consumer Culture and Postmodernism*, London: Sage.

Fox, E.J. (2018) *Born Trump: Inside America's First Family*, New York: Harper.

Frances, A. (2013) *Saving Normal: An Insider's Revolt against Out-Of-Control Psychiatric Diagnosis, DSM-5, Big Pharma, and the Medicalization of Ordinary life*, New York: HarperCollins (William Morrow).

Freud, S. (2010[1931]) *The Interpretation of Dreams: The Complete and Definitive Text*, New York: Basic Books.

Freud, S. (1949) *Group Psychology and the Analysis of the Ego*, London: The Hogarth Press.

Freud, S. (1957) *Civilization and its Discontents*, London: The Hogarth Press.

Frum, D. (2018) *Trumpocracy: The Corruption of the American Republic*, New York: Harper.

Gallup, G.H. and Rae, S.F. (1968) *The pulse of democracy: the public-opinion poll and how it works*, Santa Barbara, California: Greenwood Press.

Gartner, J., Buser, S. and Cruz, L. (eds) (2018) *Rocket Man: Nuclear Madness and the Mind of Donald Trump*, Asheville, North Carolina: Chiron Publications.

Goode, L. (2005) *Jürgen Habermas: Democracy and the Public Sphere*, London: Pluto Press.

Goodwin, N.R., Ackerman, F., and Kiron, D. (eds) (1997) *The Consumer Society*, Washington, D.C.: Island Press.

Green, J. (2017) *Devil's Bargain: Steve Bannon, Donald Trump, and the Storming of the Presidency*, New York: Penguin Press.

Habermas, J. (1989) *The Structural Transformation of the Public Sphere: An Inquiry into a Category of Bourgeois Society*, Cambridge, Massachusetts: MIT Press.

Halloran, J.D. (1993) "The European Image: Unity in Diversity – Myth or Reality," A Presentation at the IAMCR Conference, Dublin, June 1993.

Harding, L. (2017) *Collusion: Secret Meetings, Dirty Money, and How Russia Helped Donald Trump Win*, New York: Vintage Books.

Harrison, T. (2011[1976]) *Living Through the Blitz (Mass Observation Social Surveys)*, London: Faber and Faber.

Harrison, T. and Madge, C. (1987) *Britain: By Mass-Observation*, Exeter: David & Charles.

Hayden, M.V. (2018) *The Assault on Intelligence: American National Security in an Age of Lies*, New York: Penguin Press.

Herman, E.S. and Chomsky, N. (1988) *Manufacturing Consent: The Political Economy of the Mass Media*, New York: Pantheon Books.

Hubble, N. (2006) *Mass-Observation and Everyday Life: Culture, History, Theory*, Houndmills, Basingstoke: Palgrave MacMillan.

Isikoff, M. and Corn, D. (2018) *Russian Roulette: The Inside Story of Putin's War on America and the Election of Donald Trump*, New York: Twelve.

Jarrett, G. (2018) *The Russia Hoax: The Illicit Scheme to Clear Hillary Clinton and Frame Donald Trump*, New York: Broadside Books.

Johnson, P. (2006) *Habermas: Rescuing the Public Sphere*, London: Routledge.

Johnston, D.C. (2016) *The Making of Donald Trump*, Brooklyn: Melville House.

Jones, P.d'A. (1965) *The Consumer Society: A History of American Capitalism*, Harmondsworth, Middlesex: Penguin Books.

Klaas, B. (2017) *The Despot's Apprentice: Donald Trump's Attack on Democracy*, London: C. Hurst and Co.

Koffler, K. (2017) *Bannon: Always the Rebel*, Washington, D.C.: Regnery Publishing.

Kunczik, M. (1993) *Communication and Social Change*, Bonn: FES.

Kuntsman, A. (ed.) (2017) *Selfie Citizenship*, New York: Palgrave Macmillan.

Lakhani, D. (2008) *Subliminal Persuasion: Influence & Marketing Secrets They Don't Want You To Know*, Hoboken, New Jersey: John Wiley & Sons, Inc.

Laterza, V. (2018) "Cambridge Analytica, independent research and the national interest", *Anthropology Today*, Vol. 34(3): 1–2.

Lee, B.X., Lifton, R.J. and Sheehy, G. (2017) *The Dangerous Case of Donald Trump: 27 Psychiatrists and Mental Health Experts Assess a President*, New York: Thomas Dunne Books.

Lerner, D. (1958) *The Passing of Traditional Society: Modernizing the Middle East*, New York: The Free Press.

Lewandowski, C.R. and Bossie, D.N. (2018) *Let Trump Be Trump: The Inside Story of His Rise to the Presidency*, New York: Center Street.

Lynn, J. and Jay, A. (eds) (1989) *The Complete Yes Prime Minister: The Diaries of the Right Hon. James Hacker*, London: BBC Books.

Machiavelli, N. (1992) *The Prince*, New York: Dover Publications.

Marcotte, A. (2018) *Troll Nation: How The Right Became Trump-Worshipping Monsters Set On Rat-F*cking Liberals, America, and Truth Itself*, New York: Skyhorse Publishing.

Marcuse, H. (2002[1964]) *One Dimensional Man: Studies in the Ideology of Advanced Industrial Society*, London: Routledge.

McCain, J. (2018) *The Restless Wave: Good Times, Just Causes, Great Fights, and Other Appreciations*, New York: Simon & Schuster.

McChesney, R.W. (2013) *Digital Disconnect: How Capitalism Is Turning the Internet against Democracy*, New York: The New Press.

McChesney, R.W. (2015) *Rich Media, Poor Democracy: Communication Politics in Dubious Times*, New York: The New Press.

McChesney, R.W. and Nichols, J. (2016) *People Get Ready: The Fight Against a Jobless Economy and a Citizenless Democracy*, New York: Nation Books.

Mcfaul, M. (2018) *From Cold War to Hot Peace: An American Ambassador in Putin's Russia*, New York: Houghton Mifflin Harcourt.

Meacham, J. (2018) *The Soul of America: The Battle for Our Better Angels*, New York: Random House.

Miller, D. (ed.) (1995) *Acknowledging Consumption: A Review of New Studies*, London: Routledge.

Miller, D. (2012) *Consumption and Its Consequences*, Cambridge: Polity.

Mills, C.W. (1956) *The Power Elite*, Oxford: Oxford University Press.

Nance, M. (2018) *The Plot to Destroy Democracy: How Putin and His Spies Are Undermining America and Dismantling the West*, New York: Hachette Books.

Newport, F., Jones, J.M., Saad, L., Gallup, A.M. and Israel, F.L. (2009) *Winning the White House 2008: The Gallup Poll, Public Opinion, and the Presidency*, New York: Infobase Publishing.

Nichols, J. and McChesney, R.W. (2013) *Dollarocracy: How the Money and Media Election Complex is Destroying America*, New York: Nation Books.

Nyamnjoh, F.B. (2005) *Africa's Media: Democracy and the Politics of Belonging*, London: Zed Books.

Nyamnjoh, F.B. (2015) *C'est l'homme qui fait l'homme: Cul-de-Sac Ubuntu-ism in Côte d'Ivoire*, Bamenda: Langaa.

Nyamnjoh, F.B. (2016) *#RhodesMustFall: Nibbling at Resilient Colonialism in South Africa*, Bamenda: Langaa.

Nyamnjoh, F.B. (2017a) *Drinking from the Cosmic Gourd: How Amos Tutuola Can Change Our Minds*, Bamenda: Langaa.

Nyamnjoh, F.B. (2017[2015]b) "Incompleteness: Frontier Africa and the Currency of Conviviality", *Journal of Asian and African Studies*, Vol. 52(3): 253–270.

O'Brien, T.L. (2016[2007]) *TrumpNation: The Art of Being The Donald*, New York: Grand Central Publishing.

Ohmer, S. (2006) *George Gallup in Hollywood*, New York: Columbia University Press.

Packard, V., (1981[1957]) *The Hidden Persuaders*, Harmondsworth, Middlesex: Penguin Books.

Pirro, J.J. (2018) *Liars, Leakers, and Liberals: The Case Against the Anti-Trump Conspiracy*, New York: Hachette Books.

Raymond, A. with Spiegelman, I. (2008) *How to Rig an Election: Confessions of a Republican Operative*, New York: Simon & Schuster.

Reich, W., (1946) *The Mass Psychology of Fascism*, New York: Orgone Institute Press.

Ross, G.H., with McLean, A.J. (2005) *Trump Strategies for Real Estate: Billionaire Lessons for Small Investors*, Hoboken, New Jersey: John Wiley & Sons, Inc.

Sanger, D.E. (2018) *The Perfect Weapon: War, Sabotage, and Fear in the Cyber Age*, London: Scribe Publications.

Schramm, W. (1964) *Mass Media and National Development: The Role of Information in the Developing Countries*. Stanford: Stanford University Press.

Sherman, G. (2017) *The Loudest Voice in the Room: How the Brilliant, Bombastic Roger Ailes Built Fox News – and Divided a Country*, New York: Random House Trade Paperbacks.

Snyder, T. (2017) *On Tyranny: Twenty Lessons from the Twentieth Century*, New York: Tim Duggan Books.

Snyder, T. (2018) *The Road to Unfreedom: Russia, Europe, America*, New York: Tim Duggan Books.

Spicer, S. (2018) *The Briefing: Politics, The Press, and The President*, Washington, D.C.: Regnery Publishing.

Stephens-Davidowitz, S. (2017) *Everybody Lies: Big Data, New Data, and What the Internet Can Tell Us About Who We Really Are*, New York: Dey Street Books.

Stevenson, R.L. (2017[1886]) *Strange Case of Dr Jekyll and Mr Hyde*, CreateSpace Independent Publishing Platform.

Stewart-Steinberg, S. (2011) *Impious Fidelity: Anna Freud, Psychoanalysis, Politics*, Ithaca: Cornell University Press.

Storr, W. (2018) *Selfie: How We Became So Self-Obsessed and What It's Doing To Us*, New York: The Overlook Press.

The Daily Show, with Noah, T. and Meacham, J. (2018) *The Donald J. Trump Presidential Twitter Library*, New York: Spiegel & Grau.

The F. W. Faxon Company (1951) *Public Relations, Edward L. Bernays and the American Scene: Annotated Bibliography of and Reference Guide to Writings By and About Edward L. Bernays from 1917 to 1951*, Concord, New Hampshire: Rumford Press.

Trump, D.J. with McIver, M. and Kiyosaki, R.T. with Lechter, S. (2006) *Why We Want You to Be Rich: Two Men. One Message*, New York: Rich Press.

Trump, D.J. with McIver, M. (2007) *101: The Way to Success*, Hoboken, New Jersey: John Wiley & Sons, Inc.

Trump, D.J. with McIver, M. (2008) *Never Give Up: How I Turned My Biggest Challenge into Success*, Hoboken, New Jersey: John Wiley & Sons, Inc.

Trump, D.J. with Schwartz, T. (1987) *The Art of the Deal*, New York: Ballantine Books.

Tye, L. (1998) *The Father of Spin: Edward L. Bernays and the Birth of Public Relations*, New York: Crown Publishers.

Wapshott, N. (2007) *Ronald Reagan and Margaret Thatcher: A Political Marriage*, London: Sentinel (Penguin).

Watts, C. (2018) *Messing with the Enemy: Surviving in a Social Media World of Hackers, Terrorists, Russians, and Fake News*, New York: Harper.

Williams, A.D. (ed.) (2001) *The Essential Galbraith: John Kenneth Galbraith*, Boston: Houghton Mifflin Company.

Wilson, R. (2018) *Everything Trump Touches Dies: A Republican Strategist Gets Real About the Worst President Ever*, New York: Free Press.

Wiskemann, E. (1966) *Europe of the Dictators: 1919–1945*, Manchester: Collins.

Wolff, M. (2018) *Fire and Fury: Inside the Trump White House*, London: Little, Brown.

Wong, C.J. (2010) *Boundaries of Obligation in American Politics: Geographic, National, and Racial Communities*, Cambridge: Cambridge University Press.

Zola, E. (2008[1883]) *The Ladies' Paradise*, Oxford: Oxford University Press.

134

Afterword

Jean-Pierre Warnier

Francis Nyamnjoh tackles with remarkable boldness the debate over the rational choice theory and its opposite, the Bernays pseudo-Freudian propaganda based on individual unconscious irrational drives, and connects it with the Cambridge Analytica and Facebook debates. His rather optimistic conclusion concerning Trump is encouraging. While agreeing on the general overtone of his essay, I can contribute by raising two issues.

1. Bernays and psychoanalysis

Bernays was an extremely clever, intelligent, cynical and opportunistic operator. What he did for the development of "propaganda" into "public relations" can be summarised as follows: he saw the potential of the new communication technologies of the time – radio and cinema – for propaganda. Second, he understood that he had to dress up propaganda into a new, enticing, scientific jargon. Psychoanalysis came in handy at the right time and at the right place.

In the period under consideration, psychoanalysis was very much in the making, and an extremely complex affair, all the more for people who did not belong to the inner circle of its European creators who, at the time, were exclusively medical doctors. Lay psychoanalysis had not started yet. Bernays, who was not an MD, knew next to nothing about the innovations brought about by his uncle. The fact that he was Sigmund Freud's nephew and that he was in charge of collecting his royalties in the US did not qualify him as a psychoanalyst. He did not belong to any of the analytical societies founded in the wake of Freud, Jung and Ferenczi's trip to the USA in 1909 like the American Psychoanalytical Association and the NY Psychoanalytic Society. He picked up a couple of notions like the unconscious as repressed, drives, complexes and the phallus. He had a clear sense of the fact that psychoanalysis was new in the USA, that it was said to be highly scientific, that there was a fad about it, and that he could put vulgar psychoanalysis to good use by casting old propaganda recipes in a brand new (fake) discourse. It was so crude that, by so doing, he contributed in the long run to the discredit of psychoanalysis in the USA.

Bernays's use of vulgar psychoanalysis would not deserve a debate, except that it obscures the question of rational choice, and it has the paradoxical effect of reinforcing the grip of capitalistic pharma-giants on mental health programmes. Let me explain.

Freud's main discovery was that of the unconscious as repressed, that is, the fact that unsavoury, painful affects, ideas and events tend to be pushed under the carpet by the subject. If not, each and every human being would be overwhelmed by negative things to the point of paralysis. It is a normal and useful process. Not a pathological one. I will not address here the question of the validation of this discovery.

Most importantly, *contra* Bernays, the opposition between the unconscious as repressedversus conscious affects and ideas does not fit with the opposition between irrational vs rational thought. Unbearable rational thoughts are eligible for repression and to being pushed under the unconscious carpet. The scientific rationality of race equality, climate change and Darwinian evolution are unbearable to the Klu-Klux-Clan, Donald Trump and his evangelical supporters who are likely to push them back into their own individual unconscious as unbearable (rational) thoughts. We would be right to conclude that the contents of their unconscious as repressed is replete with rational, scientific knowledge they have no desire to

136

contemplate. The psychoanalytical cure consists in slowly lifting the defence mechanisms of the subject so as to unearth the painful contents that have been repressed. In a nutshell, within the confines of the unconscious, there are irrational *and* rational contents, and it is exactly the same with the conscious ego that entertains rational *and* irrational thoughts and affects. In that respect, the whole of Bernays's construction falls down into pieces. The success of Bernays is not predicated on psychoanalysis but on something else.

True enough, the notion of the unconscious does not provide the toolkit that would be needed to analyse, let alone to cure the psychic sufferings of the subject. The notions of super-ego, the distinction between psychotic and neurotic ailments, the notion of defence mechanisms, of displacement, of the subject, of symbolic division, etc. are all needed to generate the theoretical framework of psychoanalysis. In addition to the construction of this theoretical framework, it took the whole 20th century to accumulate the practical experience and expertise of the cure and assess its limitations and potential. It is clearly relevant in a number of psychic conditions, but certainly not in the case of most psychoses and genetically determined ailments.

Bernays needed a new vocabulary to disguise the old propaganda wolf under the sheepskin of a scientific-looking discourse. At the time, it looked like psychoanalysis was a genuine scientific innovation. Freud himself was partly responsible for this state of affairs. He himself was a medical doctor and insisted on grounding psychoanalysis into the neuro-physiological sciences to establish its scientific credentials, whereas its genealogy, as established by a number of scholars, including J. Lacan, Jean Allouch and Michel Foucault, was reassessed in the late 20th century and connected to the spiritual traditions of the East and the West[1] and *not* to the neuro-sciences. Freud mislead his nephew, Bernays, with the effect that, in the long run, psychoanalysis became an easy target for all its enemies from various quarters – those who, for religious or ideological reasons reject its potential for personal liberation and for social and political critique, and those who, for the same reasons and for economic ones, want to establish a monopoly of medical psychiatry on psychic sufferings and respond to them by prescribing and selling drugs. Medical psychiatry is more profitable than psychoanalysis for the pharmaceutical industry. It brings more money than does addressing oppression, repression, class trauma and issues of inequality through the speech cure that does not lend itself to a capitalistic, industrial approach, whereas medical psychiatry is wide open to capitalistic entrepreneurship through commercial clinics and the pharma-business, together with "public relations", lobbying and commercials in specialised media and social networks. By contrast, psychoanalysis is not amenable to a capitalistic organisation. This is why so many people have a vested interest in trying to disqualify Freud's innovations both in Europe and in the USA. This first debate is by no means extraneous to the Bernays case, and the documentary films recently produced on the supposed implication of psychoanalysis in the origins of "public relations", alias propaganda, are one more piece of disinformation to be added to the many publications against psychoanalysis in recent years.[2]

The first American psychoanalysts were quick in addressing issues of class struggle and the predicament of formerly enslaved persons and of Amerindians. Abram Kardiner addressed both issues. Georges Devereux the second one (see his *Psychothérapie d'un Indien des Plaines*, that was turned into a movie a few years ago).[3] If this is true, I do not think that one can talk of American psychoanalysts as a single, homogeneous, category. They were extremely diverse. Because I patronised the couch for some 12 years, and given my knowledge of what Freud stands for, I think that there is a real debate on psychoanalysis in the USA that deserves a better treatment

138

than given around the Bernays case. There is one more thing to it: since the 1940s, American psychiatrists (that is, medical doctors who are not psychoanalysts but address the question of mental illness) work hand in hand with the pharma giants who subsidise the production of the DSM[4] (now DSM 5), that is, the psychiatric textbook that classifies mental illnesses and, for each of them, proposes the appropriate pharmaceutical treatment. Bingo! As a result, in the USA, the population suffers from overmedication and overdoses of various drugs. In France, it is a big issue, and psychoanalysts fight against the pharmaceutical industry and its lobbies, at least for those of their patients who respond to the psychoanalytical cure (not all of them by far). And the pharma giants respond with equivalent attacks on psychoanalysis, but with their own – much more powerful – financial and lobbying means.

Nyamnjoh's essay raises this first debate. It concerns psychoanalysis (and Bernays). In my view, Bernays's use of psychoanalysis is purely opportunistic, and this use should be exposed for what it is and for its implications. What makes good storytelling does not necessarily make good scholarship. Bernays's contribution was immense, but it consisted in taking stock of technological innovations such as the cinema and the radio to be put to use for political purposes, and of the potential for new consumption habits in the USA, and in using the olds tricks of propaganda to cast them into a new vocabulary and new technologies. Plus, over the last 15 years, say, since 2000, the scientific domain that is behind the propaganda and advert technologies is the cognitive neurosciences, especially the so-called "social neurosciences". They are being coupled with new technologies, the internet and social networks. Forget about psychoanalysis. Tye's book in 1998 puts Bernays back on the front stage, and together with him, psychoanalysis. But it may very well be anachronistic as regards developments in public relations.[5]

In documentaries such as the ones produced by the BBC and by ARTE, I miss a number of things. The first one is a robust historical approach of propaganda, especially political, in relation to the controversial question of crowd psychology (*à la* Le Bon). There has been a good deal of historical research on, for example, the French revolution, the role of the printed press, of think tanks, of the dynamics between the educated elites and their more popular networks. Augustin Cochin is one of the early historians who tackled those issues, and his work is being revisited.[6] In the context of long-term history, Bernays would appear for what he is: a technological innovator on a background of very long-term social and political dynamics.

The other thing I miss in those documentaries is the possible contribution of robust historical research on consumption. People like Daniel Roche in France have established that mass consumption began in the mid-18th century, especially in textiles, and that the industrial revolution that was credited to innovations in the production process may have been due, in fact, to considerable changes in consumption patterns. Dany Miller has put that sort of historical literature to good use.[7]

2. The philosophical debate

The second debate raised by Nyamnjoh's essay is a philosophical one. The question of the *individual* (credited with rational choice and competitive logics *à la* Reagan/Thatcher, or else with irrational unconscious drives that can be manipulated *à la* Bernays) is a construction that belongs with philosophical anthropology. Of late, it has been included under the blanket terms of ontology or epistemology. Either one, it does not matter very much.

What is a human being? What is a human being as against an inanimate being, an animal, a spirit, etc.? Is it a choice-making *individual* (whether basically rational or irrational) or a *subject,* that is, at the same time subjected and self-governing *à la* Zizek/Foucault, or else again a *person à la* Mauss? Or something else again? Western philosophy has addressed this very question since antiquity and the social and human sciences did it since their very foundation in the 18th century. In the West, the human and social sciences grew up at the expense of philosophy and often against it, to the extent that most social scientists (and economists are the worst of all in that respect) tend to think that they can answer the question of "what is a human being" without the help of philosophy. This, in my view, is impossible. Human and social sciences cannot do without philosophy, especially concerning the question of what is a human being.

Two events have radically altered the terms of the debate. The first one is the very development of the human and social sciences in a space formerly occupied by philosophy. The second one is the globalisation of this field of enquiry. It is not any longer the preserve of Western, Cartesian and Kantian philosophy or of the social sciences. It is a global issue for humanity. The first one has expelled philosophy from its centrality in the Western world and replaced it by mostly by the so-called "economic science" and its self-managing, rational, egotistic, individual. The second one has expelled Western thought from its centrality and replaced it – it seems to me – by nothing worth mentioning. The challenge is now to construct a global philosophical anthropology attuned to researches in the social and human sciences all over the world and with various local traditions in Africa, Asia, the Americas and Europe.

If I were much younger than I am, I would launch a research programme in comparative philosophical anthropology all over the world. The question is: is there any kind of conceptual common denominator we could all agree upon in the different cultural traditions of the world? Could this common denominator provide the social sciences with a notion of the human being that could dislodge the self-managing individual puppet of global economic science from its centrality, and that would procure a philosophical reference to human rights less narrow and less Eurocentric than the legal tradition of the European Enlightenment? In anthropology, the "ontological turn" has gone a long way in that direction as well as a number of attempts made under the epistemological banner.

To those attempts, I would add one more: I would take my clue from quite different sources and not only the cultural traditions of given peoples in the anthropological sense of the term. I would tap religious and spiritual traditions, philosophy, but perhaps most importantly, contemporary literature. It strikes me that a number of authors, all around the world, share common themes central to a philosophical anthropology: I would conduct a cross-cultural comparative enquiry on authors like Tutuola, Murakami, Klosowski, Foucault and others to see if one can sketch a philosophical anthropology that is shared by quite different people across the world. I would need a Chinese author, an Indian one, an Arabic one. The sketch would be very close to Tutuola's incompleteness as very well developed and theorised by Nyamnjoh.[8] I think it might be much easier than we think and it would expel the Western rational individual from its central position in the social sciences and the neoliberal complex.

The question of consent raised by Bernays (consent induced by the manipulation of unconscious drives or by rational thought) is a philosophical one. In that respect, I am a starch Foucauldian: human beings cannot be adequately defined as *individuals* but as *subjects*, who take themselves as objects of their own actions while being subjected to other people's actions on themselves that amount to a sovereignty. This is not peculiar to large-scale so-called modern societies. It is true even among small bands of Pygmies. To go back to one of the most striking actions of Bernays, in the case of women who are banned from smoking, in order to turn them into smokers, right from the start, you need women who are *subjects* of their own desires and actions and who, beforehand, exercise techniques of the self, such as being consumers of cosmetics, dress, food etc. If not, you cannot turn them into smokers.

Together with Foucault, I would take Lacan on board, who has strongly dismissed any claim of psychoanalysis at being a science or even a knowledge.[9] For him (and I agree) it was a kind of spiritual practice. His (one time) friend Foucault, agreed on that. In the context of that philosophical debate, the question of rationality/irrationality is irrelevant.

Descartes and his incarnated *cogito* as the last truth on the subject is now out of the way. The subject is something more elusive, divided, incomplete. It never knows exactly where it stands. Neither do we. It is not an essence but an event. It may happen or not. It may come into being and disappear. There may be processes of subjectivation and de-subjectivation. This is what I read in the novels of Murakami, Tutuola and Klossowski. For sure, with a critical look at world literature, one could find many other similar leads.

Paris
July 2018

Notes

[1] On the genealogy of psychoanalysis – scientific or spiritual – see J.-P. Warnier, "Foucault usager de Lacan. Ou comment penser le sujet mais autrement", in P. Hintermeyer (ed.) *Foucault post mortem en Europe*, Strasbourg, Presses Universitaires de Strasbourg, 2015, pp. 21–30, that provides a summary of the debate.

[2] For an example, see the highly controversial but widely advertised *Le Livre noir de la psychanalyse: Vivre, penser et aller mieux sans Freud*, C. Meyer (ed.), Paris, Les Arènes, 2005.

[3] Georges Devereux, *Psychothérapie d'un Indien des plaines: réalité et rêve*, Paris, Fayard, 1998, trad. from *Reality and Dream*, New York, 1951, film *Jimmy P.*, by A. Deplechin, Fr., 2013; A. Kardiner, *The Mark of Oppression. A Psychological Study of the American Negro*, New York: Columbia University Press, 1951.

[4] *Diagnostic and Statistical Manual of Mental Disorders* (DSM) of the American Psychiatric Association, now in its fifth edition.

[5] I have not watched the BBC documentaries, but I saw the ARTE TV equivalent on Bernays, that is, "Propaganda. La fabrique du consentement" by Jimmy Leipold, 2017. It is part of a series of ten documentaries on propaganda. I have not seen the other nine. It skips psychoanalysis without any loss of information about the innovations brought about by Bernays.

[6] F. E. Schrader, *Augustin Cochin et la République française*, Paris, Seuil, 1992.

[7] D. Roche. *Histoire des choses banales: naissance de la consommation dans les sociétés traditionnelles, XVIIe-XIXe siècle*, Paris, Fayard, 1997.

[8] See F. B. Nyamnjoh, (2017) *Drinking from the Cosmic Gourd: How Amos Tutuola Can Change Our Minds*, Bamenda: Langaa.

[9] On Foucault, Lacan, psychoanalysis and the philosophical question of the subject, see J.-P. Warnier, "Foucault, usager de Lacan. Ou comment penser le sujet, mais autrement", in Pascal Hintermeyer (ed.), *Foucault post mortem en Europe*, Strasbourg, Presses Universitaires de Strasbourg, 2015, pp. 21–30.

Index

Z

Printed in the United States
By Bookmasters